C000093988

ARCHITECTURAL
The Journal of the Architectural Heritage Society of Scotland
HERITAGE I

~

WILLIAM ADAM

~

EDINBURGH
University Press
1990

The Architectural Heritage Society of Scotland
43b Manor Place, Edinburgh EH3 7EB
Tel. (031) 225 9724

Manuscripts for submission to *Architectural Heritage* should be sent to the Editor, Dr Deborah Howard, Department of Architecture, University of Edinburgh, 20 Chambers Street, Edinburgh EH1 1JZ.

Architectural Heritage I is the seventeenth issue of *The Journal of the Architectural Heritage Society of Scotland* (formerly *The Scottish Georgian Society*). Backnumbers (1, 7–11, 13, 15, 16) are available from the Society.

© The Architectural Heritage Society
of Scotland

Edinburgh University Press
22 George Square, Edinburgh

Set in Lasercomp Perpetua
and printed in Great Britain by
The Alden Press Ltd,
London and Oxford

British Library Cataloguing
in Publication Data
Architectural heritage.
 1–
 1. Great Britain. Architecture, history
720.941

ISBN 0 7486 0232 1

CONTENTS

THIS issue of the Journal of the Architectural Heritage Society of Scotland publishes the proceedings of the outstandingly successful conference on *William Adam* held at Hopetoun House on 28 October 1989, as part of the architect's Tercentenary celebrations.

This symposium, attended by almost 300 delegates, showed that William Adam's richly eclectic style was a convincing and meaningful alternative to the dogmatic Palladianism then beginning to prevail in England. The papers published in this volume add many new dimensions to our understanding of William Adam himself and of his legacy to his architect sons, John, Robert and James.

The publication has been generously sponsored by the Samuel H. Kress Foundation, the Paul Mellon Centre for British Art and the British Academy.

This issue is dedicated to the memory of
ERIC IVORY 1906 – 88
late president of the society

JOHN GIFFORD

William Adam and the Historians

William Adam was accepted in the eighteenth and early nineteenth centuries as the pre-eminent Scottish architect of his generation. In the late nineteenth and early twentieth centuries his work came to be viewed by Scots as unScottish and by English as of interest primarily because he had fathered Robert and James Adam. Recent scholars have begun to stress his Scottishness and his importance as the dominant architectural figure of his time.

WRITERS of the eighteenth and early nineteenth centuries accepted unquestioningly John Clerk of Eldin's evaluation of William Adam as the 'universal architect of this country [Scotland].'[1] In an unusually fulsome obituary *The Caledonian Mercury* of 30 June 1748 stated that 'his Genius for Architecture push'd him out of Obscurity into a high Degree of Reputation'.[2] During his tour of Scotland twelve years later Bishop Richard Pococke noted in his journal that Dundee Town House had been 'built by Adam the Architect' and that Yester House was 'the architecture of old Adams'.[3] About the same time Sir Robert Douglas of Glenbervie wrote that William Adam, 'having applied himself to architecture, became so eminent in his profession, that in his time he had no equal in this country. . .'[4] Such a judgment was given support by John Woolfe and James Gandon whose fifth volume of *Vitruvius Britannicus*, published in 1771, illustrated only one Scottish building, William Adam's Duff House, albeit with wings designed by Woolfe and Gandon.[5] Further publicity was given to the work of Adam in 1780 when Thomas Cordiner mentioned the *Vitruvius Britannicus* plates as showing a work 'of the late celebrated Mr *Adams*'.[6] As late as 1830 *The Edinburgh Encyclopaedia*'s article on Robert Adam stated that:

> . . .The genius of his father, William Adam of Maryburgh in Fife, was eminently conspicuous in Hopetoun House, in the Royal Infirmary, and in other buildings, both public and private.[7]

The mid-nineteenth-century revival of interest in the architecture of tower houses, whose details were used to provide Scottish Baronial clothing for country houses, banks and town halls, found its scholarly summation in David MacGibbon and Thomas Ross's five volumes on *The Castellated and Domestic Architecture of Scotland* (1887–92). Originally MacGibbon and Ross had intended a two-volume history illustrated with plentiful examples, and it was only at a late stage that they decided to expand this by a further three volumes to make a comprehensive inventory of Scottish secular architecture. The last building described in their second volume, and thus originally intended as the final work mentioned in their history, was William Adam's The Drum of which they wrote:

> With this mansion we close for the present our review of the Domestic Architecture of Scotland, and we select this edifice for that purpose, as it is a favourable example of the completely developed Renaissance style, in which not a single reminiscence of the Scottish forms and features is to be found. We might have chosen far larger and more imposing examples, but could hardly have found one where the spirit of the Renaissance is carried out with greater refinement and beauty of detail. . .[8]

This evaluation of The Drum, surprisingly eulogistic to a classical purist, made of William Adam's work a gravestone marking the demise of *Scottish* architecture. After noting that earlier buildings had displayed 'Renaissance' or classical detail, MacGibbon and Ross continued:

> But these are all influenced more or less by the spirit of Scottish art. At Drum all traces of this native style have disappeared, and its architect, we can easily see, drew his inspiration from buildings entirely 'furth of Scotland'.[9]

At the same time as they argued that Adam's architecture marked a final break with the 'native style', MacGibbon and Ross applauded his genius as a classicist with their description of *Vitruvius Scoticus*:

> In looking at the designs in this volume, one would almost fancy he was turning over the pages of 'Palladio'. His fame has been eclipsed by that of his sons, but it is open to doubt if he was not at least their equal.[10]

MacGibbon and Ross's view of William Adam was remarkably persistent in Scotland. As late as 1965 W. Douglas Simpson, for long the doyen of Scottish architectural historians, found William Adam's design for Haddo House:

> . . .a brilliantly successful essay in the pure Palladian style: and with this, we may see that the native Scottish manner has finally given way to the architectural modes of contemporary western Europe.[11]

English historians' awareness of William Adam stemmed from the Adam Revival of the later nineteenth century and for them William Adam's interest lay in his having fathered Robert and James and in the contrast which could be drawn between his work and theirs. John Swarbrick in *Robert Adam & his Brothers* of 1915 dismissed William Adam as 'a strict Palladian',[12] a description of doubtful exactitude but sufficient to distinguish the father from his sons. In the same year *Country Life* published an article on The Drum by Arthur T. Bolton, Curator of Sir John Soane's Museum and thus of the bulk of Robert and James Adam's architectural drawings. Bolton introduced William ('the father of the more famous Adelphi brethren') as the author of *Vitruvius Scoticus* but hardly found that a cause of commendation:

> The main impression produced is that of a solid, stodgy mass of work, painstaking and thorough, but disclosing few ideas and little originality.

William Adam seems to have been influenced by the general work of the
time, and his designs will be found to be a compilation of ideas from
various sources. He varies from Vanbrugh and Gibbs to Kent. His inside
work is particularly heavy and ordinary, and is far removed from the brilliant effectivness of his son Robert. . .

Bolton thought The Drum William Adam's 'masterpiece' but found little kind to say
about it. Its general external massing he pronounced 'very crowded' and the pedimented
centrepiece 'over-accentuated with rustication, in a way which destroys the effect of the
fluted and banded pilasters at the angles'. By contrast:

The garden front suggests that William Adam would have succeeded better
with the simple classic, free of the orders of which he had no real grasp.

The Drum's interior pleased Bolton little more. The entrance hall ('the most
successfully decorated feature of the house'):

. . .has all the full bodied richness of the Early Georgian. There is the
flavour of the Low Countries where, as the old saying tells us, the English
solidiers learnt to swear horribly, and equally, we may presume, the
artists learnt to be profuse.

The family dining room he thought 'even more profuse, but less successful, owing to
a defective scale and overcrowded features'. The overmantel of the drawing room
(originally the state dining room) was 'a work like that for which, in Kipling's story,
Torregiano administers severe chastisement on his English pupil'. In conclusion:

'The interiors of the Drum are, in fact, explanatory of Robert Adam's
prefaces, in which he inveighs against the crudeness of the interior decoration of the previous generation.'[3]

With the publication in 1922 of The Architecture of Robert & James Adam Bolton's
evaluation of their father gained added authority. William Adam's work is described in
the opening pages which repeat almost word for word Bolton's Country Life article but
with a final and damning summing up:

On the face of it there is nothing in the work of William Adam senior
(1688–1748), in the main, thorough, sound and traditional, that accounts
for the exceptional gifts of his brilliant second son.[4]

Bolton's estimation of William Adam was influential. In 1932 the writer of an
unsigned article in Country Life praised the dining room (originally the entrance hall) of
Yester House as 'Burlingtonian in its restraint and elegance' but thought it necessary to
explain that it was:

representative of the elder Adam's latest period when the crudeness and
profusion we associate with his interiors have given place to a more
elegant and refined treatment. . .[5]

In 1934 Ian C. Hannah in his Story of Scotland in Stone dismissed Adam as:

'a rather ordinary classic architect whose fame has been completely over-
shadowed by that of his sons.'[6]

A *caveat* to the argument that in the early twentieth century William Adam was dismissed as a crude and second-rate architect is provided by evidence that his work was an inspiration for some architects and their clients. Motifs from plasterwork of Adam's houses were incorporated in the internal remodelling of Dunrobin Castle by Sir Robert Lorimer in 1919–21. At Lawers House William Black extended Adam's decorative scheme in about 1920.[17] In 1944 Sir John Stirling Maxwell, Chairman of the Ancient Monuments Board for Scotland and owner of Pollok House (then thought to be by William Adam), wrote to Reginald Fairlie about the design of a new shooting lodge at Corrour:

> My idea is that the new house should be the sort of thing that William Adam might have built for Lord Huntly, then owner of Corrour, if he had ordered a shooting lodge to be built on this site as he very well might have done.[18]

A serious re-evaluation of William Adam's work might have been expected in John Summerson's *Architecture in Britain, 1530–1830*, first published in 1953. However, Summerson, in dealing with the early eighteenth century, was primarily concerned with tracing the development of a Palladian orthodoxy. William Adam, hardly a conventional Palladian, was slotted into a short sub-section entitled 'Palladianism in Scotland' appended to the chapter on 'Palladian Permeation: the Villa'. Having decided on his slot, Summerson seems to have been annoyed that it was fitted badly by Adam, an architect influenced by Vanbrugh, Wren and Gibbs as well as the Palladians and who 'showed no desire to discriminate between them'. Rather surprisingly Summerson managed to detect a general adoption of 'Palladian plan arrangements' and to describe Adam's plasterwork as 'Rococo'. Less surprisingly he found in some of his houses 'a quaintly barbaric richness'.[19]

Much fuller consideration of William Adam's architecture, but as a contrast to that of his sons, was provided by John Fleming, first in his introduction to *Scottish Country Houses and their Gardens Open to the Public* (1953) and then in *Robert Adam and his Circle* (1962). Fleming made no attempt to pigeon-hole Adam, least of all as a Palladian, writing of his 'predilection for Vanbrughian solemnity' but also of 'an *ad hoc* improvisation from source-books, imperfectly digested'.[20] For Fleming, Adam's 'distinctive qualities and defects' were:

> . . .his vigour and romantic feeling for the drama of stone, as well as his tendency towards over-loading, enlargement and crowding of decorative features. . .[21]

In contrast to the attitude of MacGibbon and Ross or Douglas Simpson, Fleming stressed the Scottishness of Adam's architecture. The Drum he described as a 'free translation of Palladio into broad Lallans',[22] Duff House as 'some hirsute centurion: a local levy, of course, for its wild rugged grandeur is unmistakably Scottish'.[23] Although

4)

Fleming recognised Adam's dependence on English sources, he emphasised that these were handled in a highly individual manner:

> For most of his buildings have that rugged massiveness which dignified and that exuberance of surface decoration which enriched the old Scottish castles. Behind his cumbrous pediments one may often discern the skeleton of a crow-stepped gable and behind his wide Corinthian pilasters the ghost of a bartizan. Indeed, by combining his primitive conception of the classical mode with the brawny, martial qualities of his native Scottish tradition he succeeded in preserving some of the merits of both. Undeniably wild and woolly when compared with the sleek and well-groomed façades of his London contemporaries, the rich texture and robust uninhibited display of dog Latin at Duff House, for example, may yet be preferred to the suave manners and mincing gestures of a Marble Hill by Roger Morris.[24]

A serious attempt to evaluate William Adam's work without contrasting it with that of his sons or seeing it as a postscript to English architecture was made in *The Historic Architecture of Scotland* (1966) by John G. Dunbar who, in a neat reversal of the opinions of MacGibbon and Ross and Douglas Simpson, described Adam as:

> . . .the last major Scottish architect whose work was fundamentally different in character from that of contemporary designers on the other side of the Border.[25]

Dunbar followed Fleming in placing emphasis on Adam's patrons, notably the first Earl of Hopetoun and Sir John Clerk of Penicuik, but refrained from attempting an imitation of his literary style. Dunbar's evaluation acknowledged the influence of Vanbrugh and Gibbs, pointed out Adam's lack of sympathy with 'the severities of the English neo-Palladian school', recognised that a concern for making a strong first impression could sometimes lead to 'bizarre' results, but concluded that:

> '. . .some of Adam's work, on the other hand, achieved real dignity and grandeur, none was dull, and all of it displayed a robustness and directness of expression that were entirely appropriate in the intellectual climate of North Britain.'[26]

Dunbar's measured approach was followed by Howard Colvin in *A Biographical Dictionary of British Architects* (1978) although Colvin omitted from his list of Adam's works two houses (Pollok House and House of Gray) singled out for mention by Dunbar.[27] The history of the publication of *Vitruvius Scoticus*, previously claimed as a source for eighteenth-century American and Irish houses,[28] was elucidated by James Simpson in his introduction to a small-scale 'facsimile' of that work published in 1980.[29]

Much more ambitious, at least in its use of the English language, than the work of Dunbar and Colvin has been James Macaulay's reappraisal of William Adam in *The Classical Country House in Scotland, 1660–1800* (1987). There, the 'otherwise thoughtful critics' who have seen in William Adam 'a provincial master whose chief glory was to be the father of a more famous son' are reminded of the quality of Arniston, described as 'the mansion which approximates more closely to Palladian precepts than any other country-house of its period in Scotland'.[30] Not even Dr Macaulay's definition of Palladianism can quite encompass Duff House where 'one senses that Adam was never the slave of Palladianism, with its tenets of correctness, but retained a sturdy independence. . .'[31] Macaulay's consideration of the planning of Adam's houses leads to weird results, a discovery of an integral 'practicality' and 'homeliness',[32] and a complaint that the Venetian windows at The Drum and Torrance 'illuminate hall landings'[33]—in fact, the eighteenth-century state drawing room and a library or billiard room respectively. But much can be forgiven an author who is not afraid to write that:

> Adam ever retained a love for the sweeping chords of the Baroque in preference to the drier plainsong of Palladianism. . .[34]

Many will find hope in the realisation that there lives on in Scotland's architectural historians the spirit of the late William McGonagall, 'poet and tragedian' of Dundee.

NOTES

1. Scottish Record Office, GD 18/4981, [John Clerk of Eldin], 'Life of Robert Adam'.

2. *The Caledonian Mercury*, 30 June 1748.

3. Richard Pococke, *Tours in Scotland*, ed. Daniel William Kemp, Scottish History Society, Edinburgh, 1887, pp. 222, 316.

4. Robert Douglas, *The Baronage of Scotland*, Edinburgh, 1798, p. 256.

5. John Woolfe and James Gandon, *Vitruvius Britannicus*, v, [London], 1771, pls. 58–60.

6. Thomas Cordiner, *Antiquities & Scenery of the North of Scotland*, London, 1780, p. 4.

7. *The Edinburgh Encyclopaedia*, ed. David Brewster, i, Edinburgh, 1830, p. 135.

8. David MacGibbon and Thomas Ross, *The Castellated and Domestic Architecture of Scotland*, ii, Edinburgh, 1887, p. 557.

9. *Ibid.*, ii, pp. 557–8.

10. *Ibid.*, ii, p. 560.

11. W. Douglas Simpson, *The Ancient Stones of Scotland*, London, 1965, p. 240.

12. John Swarbrick, *Robert Adam & his Brothers*, London, 1915, p. 25.

13. Arthur T. Bolton, 'The Drum, Midlothian', *Country Life*, October 9, 1915, pp. 491–2.

14. Arthur T. Bolton, *The Architecture of Robert & James Adam*, i, London, 1922, p. 5.

15. 'Yester House', *Country Life*, July 30, 1932, p. 128.

16. Ian C. Hannah, *Story of Scotland in Stone*, Edinburgh, 1934, p. 306.

17. Christopher Hussey, 'Lawers, Perthshire', *Country Life*, October 10, 1925, p. 553.

18. National Monuments Record of Scotland, Sir John Stirling Maxwell to Reginald Fairlie, 2 March, 1944.

19. John Summerson, *Architecture in Britian, 1530–1830*, Harmondsworth, 1953, p. 227.

20. John Fleming, *Scottish Country Houses and their Gardens Open to the Public*, London, 1954, pp. 14–16.

21. John Fleming, *Robert Adam and his Circle*, London, 1962, p. 36.

22. *Ibid.*, p. 49.

23. *Ibid.*, p. 55.

24. *Ibid.*, p. 73.

25. John G. Dunbar, *The Historic Architecture of Scotland*, London, 1966, p. 107.

26. *Ibid.*, p. 108.

27. Howard Colvin, *A Biographical Dictionary of British Architects, 1600–1840*, London, 1978.

28. e.g. Desmond Fitzgerald, 'Nathaniel Clement and some eighteenth-century Irish Houses', *Apollo*, October, 1966; Desmond Guinness and Julius Trousdale Sadler, Jr., *The Palladian Style in England, Ireland and America*, London, 1976, p. 107.

29. *Vitruvius Scoticus*, ed. James Simpson, Edinburgh, 1980.

30. James Macaulay, *The Classical Country House in Scotland, 1660–1800*, London, 1987, p. 70.

31. *Ibid.*, p. 79.

32. *Ibid.*, p. 79.

33. *Ibid.*, p. 73.

34. *Ibid.*, p. 81.

William Adam's Library

Summary: see p. 33

IN 1979 Ian Mowat drew the attention of architectural historians to the existence of the published catalogue of the library at Blair Adam which was privately printed in 1883 and of which copies survive both in the National Libary of Scotland and at Blair Adam.[1] Mowat was careful to point out that a catalogue of books made in the late Victorian period could not provide hard evidence about the contents at any particular date of a library that had begun to be assembled perhaps some 160 years before. There was, for example, a quantity of volumes on constitutional law which most probably came to Blair Adam after what we might term its architectural period, as a result of the work of Chief Commissioner William Adam, John Adam's only surviving son, who had a distinguished parliamentary and legal career and through whom the present Adam family is descended. There were also many volumes of late Georgian literature which Mowat suggests had been bought by Commissioner Adam's daughters, and a copy of the Koran (printed in 1685) acquired no doubt in the days of Adam activity in the Indian Civil Service, so that the printed catalogue contains a great deal more than William Adam or any of his three architectural sons, John, Robert and James ever knew. But the printed Library Catalogue also contains a great many architectural books: these are assumed by Ian Mowat to have come into the library in the eighteenth century and to date back to the days when the name of Adam was synonymous with great architecture. The dates of publication support such a view, and these no doubt are the volumes that fattened out the rudimentary notions on the subject which William Adam held when, for the first time, and with the enlightened interest of the First Earl of Hopetoun, he began, in the words of his son James, seriously 'to court dame architecture' in the design of Hopetoun House.

Ian Mowat's very reasonable supposition that the architectural books were collected by William Adam and his son John has now been confirmed by the discovery at Blair Adam of an eighteenth-century manuscript list of the volumes in the library.[2] The William Adam conference seemed to offer an appropriate occasion to investigate its contents and, as it were, to turn over the pages of some of the volumes with William Adam's architecture in mind. The most recent titles date from the early 1780s. They include a work by Robert and James's pupil and some time clerk, William Thomas, *Original Designs in Architecture* of 1783 to which the Adams subscribed. The catalogue seems therefore to have been made about 1785, and its compiling at this time may very possibly be linked to the financial difficulties of the brothers' building company, William Adam & Co., and to an attempt by John Adam to obtain a valuation of this collection with a view to its sale. Blair Adam had to be put on the market at the same time but failed to find a buyer, and happily an up-turn in John Adam's affairs within a few years saved both the estate and the books in the library. Like many eighteenth-century library catalogues, the books at Blair Adam are listed directly from the shelves into the catalogue: this gives the list an evocative directness. In places it is quite tantalising when we find described, under the title Drawings, 'A large drawing book, A Book of drawings, architecture, ornaments etc., A portfolio containing plans of a house; A portfolio containing plans & sections of a bagnio; Plans of houses, gardens, pictures etc.', and 'Landscapes by several hands'. We will never know what became of this material or whether it would have illuminated further the career of William Adam or of his son John.[3]

A precise account of the contents of a library may seem a dry topic. A catalogue exists first as an aid to readers, and a mere list of titles must make dull reading. On the other hand there is something satisfying about the fact that we now know what books William Adam had to refer to as he grew in skill as an architect and what most probaby was available to his sons to feed their imaginations as young men. The correlation between a design published in one country and a piece of classical architecture in another can on occasion prove to be quite precise. If we are to understand how William Adam and his sons may have extracted ideas and inspiration from the books in their possession, it may be useful to begin with an account of some early instances of the use of pattern books in Scottish architecture. One celebrated case, first pointed out by Sir John Summerson, is the link between the plan of Heriot's Hospital in Edinburgh which Walter Balanquall, the Dean of Rochester, as one of George Heriot's trustees, had brought from England and the design for a quadrangular Renaissance chateau with an arcaded court, called Rosmarino, published in Serlio's Seventh Book. The Scottish Master Masons William Wallace and William Ayton gave the hospital some unconventional classical details, but the origins of the building are not totally disguised by these and the pattern-book source in Serlio seems secure.[4]

The west door in the courtyard that opens into the old dining hall at Heriot's provides another clear example of how a plate from a book on an architect's shelf can turn itself into stone. This is taken directly from the rusticated mannerist doorway that Vignola designed as the principal portal of the great Farnese castle of Caprarola, published in his *Regole delli Cinque Ordini* of 1562. In Vignola's design the voussoirs project boldly and break into the architrave while the keystone erupts into the frieze and projects, pendant-like, into the centre of the arch. The Scottish masons flattened or else entirely funked these bold effects but the continuous rustication across the Doric pilasters at the side leaving only the base, one rusticated block and the capital clearly expressed is copied precisely from Vignola's plate.[5] William Adam, we may note, owned many of the standard Italian pattern books of the sixteenth century: he had a French edition of Vignola and an original set of Serlio published in Paris in 1545.

9)

1. The frontispiece to Alexandre Francini's *Livre d'Architecture*, 1631.

2. The Riccarton family Monument, St Nicholas Church, Aberdeen, 1696.

One book which Adam did not apparently own is the attractive set of designs for monumental gateways published in Paris in 1631 by the Florentine architect and engineer, Alexandre Francini (Fig. 1).[6] Francini worked for Marie de Médicis, for whom he designed the Neptune fountain in the grounds of the Luxembourg Palace, and for her son Louis XIII. That his book was known and employed in Scotland is nicely demonstrated by the Mylne family monument in Greyfriars' Churchyard, Edinburgh, which copies its whole scheme, piece for piece, from the architectural frame that surrounds Francini's portrait on the title page.[7] At the top Francini has shown his coat of arms flanked by two cherubs and propped upon a grotesque face with bats' wings on either side. Free-standing columns are set on pedestals with a long tablet with an inscription in between. Mylne's Scottish cherubs are less attractive than their Gallic counterparts but the grotesque face and bats' wings are there, as are the columns, pedestal and long inscription so that we may identify clearly the Italo-French pattern book source which provided the inspiration for this seventeenth-century monument. The same plate was also used in Aberdeen for the Riccarton monument (Fig. 2) erected in St Nicholas's Churchyard in 1696 when William Adam was just seven years old. Now the grotesque face and bats' wings have gone; but the coat of arms and cherubs are still trumpeting to eternity.[8] And Francini's book provides at least one more example of direct influence–the front gate of the Argyll Lodging in Stirling, built about 1674, which reproduces precisely the rusticated piers and flat arch of the gateway illustrated in Plate 2, shorn of its broken pediment, cartouche and bust.[9]

These examples taken from Scottish architecture of the seventeenth century may serve to illustrate the type of straightforward use that might be made of a book to provide the basis for a design. When we move forward to the eighteenth century and the architecture of William Adam, the sort of neat demonstration that Francini provides is no longer possible. A far greater range of sources was available to Adam by the 1720s and 1730s and what we have to deal with now is not one source book but a whole library and a library that may be used eclectically permitting a façade to be composed from ideas in several books. While the architects of seventeenth-century Scotland are content to grab bits, a more sophisticated practice, exemplified by William Adam, tends to absorb a variety of influences, and then to render them back in changed and altered form.

The library at Blair Adam was stocked with no less than fifty-four titles of works in English on art and architecture. Of these the earliest were an anonymous *Effigies of painters and artists* (1594), John Webb's *Vindication of Stonehenge* (1665) and Sir William Dugdale's celebrated *History of St Paul's Cathedral* (1658).[10] The earliest work of regular architecture was the set of engraved designs of churches by Sir Christopher Wren, published in London without a printed text in 1718. The Adams owned most of the standard works of English Palladianism: Giacomo Leoni's translations of Palladio (1715) and Alberti (1726); the first three volumes of *Vitruvius Britannicus* (1725); William Kent's *Designs of Inigo Jones* (1727); Robert Castell's *Villas of the Ancients* (1728); Isaac Ware's *Plans, Elevations and Sections of Houghton in Norfolk* (1735) and John Vardy's *Designs of Inigo Jones and William Kent* (1744).

Considering the links between William Adam and the Earl of Mar it is hardly surprising that the library at Blair Adam also contained a complete set of the publications of James Gibbs: *A Book of Architecture* (1728); the *Rules for Drawing the Several Parts of Architecture* (1738) and the handsome single volume devoted to Gibbs's masterpiece, the Radcliffe Library in Oxford (1747). Adam also possessed one of the most widely distributed studies of comparative architecture of the period, Roland Fréart's *Parallel of Ancient and Modern Architecture* of 1733 done 'from the Frence'. Pattern book publications presenting architecture as a trade, rather than a cultural activity, are comparatively few: Batty Langley's *Young Builder's Rudiments* (1730); William Leyburn's *The Mirror of Architecture* (1735); Francis Price's *British Carpenter* (1735); three titles by William Salmon: 'Architecture'–perhaps *Palladio Londinensis* as the date given is 1734–*The Builder's Guide and Magazine of Tables* (1736) and *The London and Country Builder's Vade Mecum* (1745); and two copies of William Jones, *The Gentleman or Builder's Companion*

(1739). Rococo Gothic, a style in which John, Robert and James were all to show an early interest is represented by Langley's *Ancient Architecture Restored* (1742), by William Pain's *Builder's Companion*, which includes sixteen Gothic plates, (1758) and by Daniel Garret's *Designs and Estimates for Farmhouses* (1747) which contains some rudimentary castellated designs.

One of the more striking features of the contents of the library was the strength of its holdings of continental books. In his progress from builder to architect William Adam acquired no less than four copies of Vitruvius including an edition (1567) of the most learned of all the Latin versions with a commentary by Daniele Barbaro and plates by Palladio; the Lyon edition of 1523 and a late printing (1734) of the French translation published by Claude Perrault.[11] Adam possessed copies of Serlio (1545), Palladio (1581) and Scamozzi (1615)—all standard works for any serious architect—and, more unusually, G.A. Rusconi's neat little volume printed in Venice in 1660[12] and Guarino Guarini's *Architettura Civile* published in 1737. There are twenty-seven Italian and Latin titles in the library catalogue including eight volumes which deal with Roman antiquities.

The extent of the French literature on building is also noteworthy; the library contained no fewer than forty-five French titles. Of these Philibert De L'Orme's *Nouvelle Inventions pour Bien Batir* (1561) is the oldest. William Adam also possessed De L'Orme's *Oeuvres* in the Paris edition of 1626 and an amplified version of Pierre Le Muet, *Maniere de bien bastir*, printed in England by Robert Pricke in 1670, though the Blair Adam version was a late Parisian edition of 1681. The library contained Du Cerceau's two principal volumes, the *Livre d'architecture* (1559) and *Les plus excellents bastiments de France* (1576-79), noted in the catalogue as 'Batiments de France, Paris, 1607' and 'Architecture, Paris, 1648'; Antoine Le Pautre, *Oeuvres d'Architecture* (1652); Jean Marot *Recueil* (1676), a collection of plans of buildings in Paris and its environs; the Comte D'Aviler's *Cours d'Architecture* (1694), a meticulous compilation based on the works of Vignola and of Michelangelo; and the Abbé Cordemoy's *Nouveau traité de toute l'architecture*, one of the pioneer manifestos of rational simplicity, in an edition of 1714.

French genius had also contributed a remarkable quantity of precise technical information to the architectural and practical literature of seventeenth- and eighteenth-century Europe and, with a man of William Adam's interests and practical turn of mind, it comes as no surprise to discover that volumes of this type were widely represented by the holdings at Blair Adam. The 'Vitruvius' of this kind of literature must be George Agricola's *De Re Mettallica*, a learned treatise on metals published in Basel as twelve books with woodcut illustrations in 1621. William Adam owned a copy. He possessed copies of Abraham Bosse on engraving (1625), and on stone cutting (1643); François Derand on the construction of masonry vaults (1643), Nicholas Bion's *Traité des Instrumens de Mathematique* of 1723, a detailed account of the construction and use of mathematical instruments; and Marcel (?) Gallon's comprehensive descriptive catalogue of machines and inventions approved by the French Royal Academy of Sciences between 1648 and 1734, published in six fat volumes in 1734. After 1748 when the Adam brothers inherited their father's business in architecture, his practical interests and capacities continued to be represented in the work of his sons: such an impression certainly gathers support from the additions made to the library after William's death, for it must have been Robert Adam who bought Bernard Forest de Bélidor's *Architecture Hydraulique*, a complete work on French plumbing, published in Paris in 1753. Robert would have had an opportunity to purchase the book while in Paris at the start of his grand tour in November 1754 and, in a similar way, Claude Léopold Genneté's *Nouvelle Construction de Cheminées*, published in Liége in 1760, with the latest technology on making chimneys draw properly and preventing smoke in rooms, must have been acquired by James who, at the start of his own grand tour, passed through Belgium in May in the year in which the book came out.

A type of architectural publication which seems to have held a particular attraction for William Adam was the single volume devoted to the illustration of one important building. Adam had separate publications on the Vatican Loggia (1684), Les Invalides (1683 and 1736), Versailles (1715), sets of plates on the Hôtel of the Marquis Fontenay Marville, taken from Antoine Le Pautre, and a portfolio entitled 'French buildings, views, towns prints etc'. At some stage he also procured Jacob van Campen's volume on Amsterdam Town Hall (1664), and Paul Decker's *Architectura Civilis* (1711), a mangificent volume largely devoted to the plans for a vast Baroque Palace and some smaller hunting lodges. He also acquired a rare work in J.F. Guernery's volume on the Royal Residence of Hesse-Kassel, published in Kassel in 1706. Such evident enthusiasm for the particular delineation of famous European buildings may perhaps remind us of the young Christopher Wren fifty years before, when during his visit to Paris in 1665 he wrote, 'I have purchased a great deal of Taille-douce, in which I might give our countrymen Examples of Ornaments and Grotesks, in which the Italians confess the French to excel'.[13]

How Adam acquired these volumes is far from clear. He may have purchased standard works in Edinburgh or London and a quantity of the continental literature while abroad in the Netherlands and France. It seems unlikely, however, that the volumes on the Residence at Kassel, on Versailles or Les Invalides, which came out long after Adam had been abroad, would have been on sale in Britain, and it must be the case that these aristocratic folios were either purchased for him by a patron while abroad, or were procured from a patron at a subsequent date. In the case of the volumes by van Campen and Paul Decker, Adam seems to have retained books which, as they belonged to Lord Milton, he had no right to keep and it is not impossible that some other exotic volumes came into his collection by a similar route.[14]

Unlike his sons, William Adam did not visit Italy. Nonetheless his library catalogue contains a number of important texts on Roman antiquities: Pietro Santi Bartoli's *Antichi Sepolcri* (1697), the *Admiranda Romanorum Antiquitatum* (1685), and Giovanni Battista Cavalleri's publication on the antique statues of Rome (1585). The library also contained G.B. Falda's *Nuovo Teatro di Roma* (1665), an attractive assembly of picturesque views by Bartoli of the papal city, including engraved interiors of several Baroque churches which, at least in their drawn form, offer a hint of something of the spirit of William Adam's own grander schemes (Fig. 3). We cannot tell, however, how many of these books may have belonged to William Adam. Perhaps they were bought for John by Robert when he was in Rome and was trying to convince the elder brother of the value of his travels and even to coax a stay-at-home Johnny to follow his example and to visit Italy. There is no sure evidence. Did William Adam somehow procure Carlo Fontana's magnificent folio volume on the Colosseum, *L'Anfiteatro Flavi*, published in 1725 and containing, as well as Fontana's enthralling reconstruction of the great amphitheatre, the plans of a circular domed Baroque church which was to be erected within the ruins? Or did he purchase the five fantastical volumes of speculative classical archaeology by the sixteenth-century architect and archaeologist from Milan, Giovanni Battista Montano? Montano died in Rome in 1621 at the age of eighty-seven, and I am inclined to think that some of his volumes may indeed have been at Blair Adam during William Adam's lifetime as one of the manuscripts which Robert procured while in Italy (now preserved in the Soane Museum) is the set of original drawings prepared by Montano for this very publication.[15] If these volumes were to be found at the Blair while the brothers were growing up it is surely not fanciful to speculate on how these young men might have passed their time, on wet days, lying on the library floor of their father's house with volumes on classical antiquities all around them. It is certainly clear that the massing and intellectual qualities of a centralised plan fascinated Robert Adam throughout his life: the pattern of many of his most idealistic compositions is anticipated by many of Montano's reconstructions of ancient mausolea; while Bartoli's crisp engravings must have fuelled James's enthusiasm for 'the true taste' of Antiquity.[16]

Amongst the collection two important volumes stand out as major works of continental origin which William Adam certainly consulted. They came from the library of Andrew Fletcher, Lord Milton, a Lord of the Court of Session from 1724 and Lord Justice Clerk from 1735 to 1748. In 1740 Lord Milton evidently asked for the books to be returned to him and in reply Adam wrote 'I have sent the Book of Pallaces, that of the Stadthouse of Amsterdam I delivered back a good time ago'.[17] In writing this it seems that William Adam was mistaken, for Jacob van Campen's magnificent volume on his masterwork was still to be found in the 1780s, between a manuscript 'Book of Drawings of architecture and ornaments' and Gibson's reprint of Camden's *Britannia*, on the shelf No 38 of the Blair Adam library. About 1754 John Adam was to design a town house for Lord Milton in the Canongate in Edinburgh,[18] and we can only presume that by then

3. G.B. Falda, *Nuovo Teatro di Roma*, 1665, view of the interior of Santa Maria dell'Assunzione at Ariccia.

4. G.B. Montano, *Scielta di varii tempietti antichi*, 1624, plate 3, ideal centralised plan recon-
structed by Montano and described as an antique temple on the Via Labicana.

his patron had forgotten to check whether his father had returned the book or not and that he never asked for it back again! The *Stadthuys van Amsterdam* (1668) is one of the most handsome folio volumes on architecture ever published, with engraved text, titles and 135 plates. James Gibbs owned the book as well, and his copy, bound in pale vellum, remains with his other books in the Radcliffe Library in Oxford.[19] It seems clear that the Amsterdam Stadthaus made an impact on Adam's own architecture. The great rectangular block with its high roof, magnificent chimneys and central cupola has an austere grandeur and functional sobriety that recurs in a number of the plates in *Vitruvius Scoticus*; in its internal arrangements the building employs the pattern of an archway contained within a larger system of pilasters and entablature (Fig. 5) which was to become almost a *leitmotif* of Adam interiors;[20] and in its lavish sculptural decoration–particularly the elaborate relief panels of gods and trophies of arms in the main halls (Fig. 6)–a style of decoration is advanced which in the hands of William Clayton and other plasterers would become common in many early classical houses in Scotland.

Lord Milton's other volume, referred to by Adam as 'the Book of Pallaces', must almost certainly have been Paul Decker's *Fürstlicher Baumeister, oder: Architectura civilis*, published in Augsburg in 1711, which like the Stadthaus of Amsterdam is listed in the Blair Adam catalogue of the 1780s. Once again this is a book that was also in the collection of James Gibbs, for whom its magnificent and fantastic late Baroque idiom may have had some appeal. To William Adam the huge double plates which the book contains must have come as a revelation, for the volume consists of a series of designs for a vast Royal Palace, illustrating the most extravagant type of German Baroque architecture and decoration, its gardens and garden buildings. Two later parts to the volume (1713 and 1716), which may have been included in Lord Milton's copy, added designs for ten other houses, including a Royal palace, a town house and Lust Haus for the Margrave of Bayreuth, who had recently engaged Decker as state architect at the time of the architect's death, aged thirty-six, in 1713. If the scale and absolutist authority of Decker's courtly architecture could have no place in the Scotland of William Adam's time, the gardener in him must have responded to the panoramic views of formal gardens with symmetrical damask patterns of *parterres broderie*, clipped *allées* and formal *bosquets*. Indeed the clipped tree loggia illustrated in the second part, plate 20, almost seems to anticipate the layout of the meeting of avenues and round point at the statue of Hercules that Adam introduced into the grounds at Newliston, West Lothian in the early 1730s;[21] while the complex strapwork and illusionistic ceiling designs of the first Royal palace, though more elaborate, are not inconsistent in their individual elements with Adam's own decorative taste.

One aspect of Decker's architecture seems to have contributed directly to William Adam's own work. As Lord Milton asked about the book in 1740, we must assume that it would have been borrowed by Adam not earlier than the 1730s. This means that the

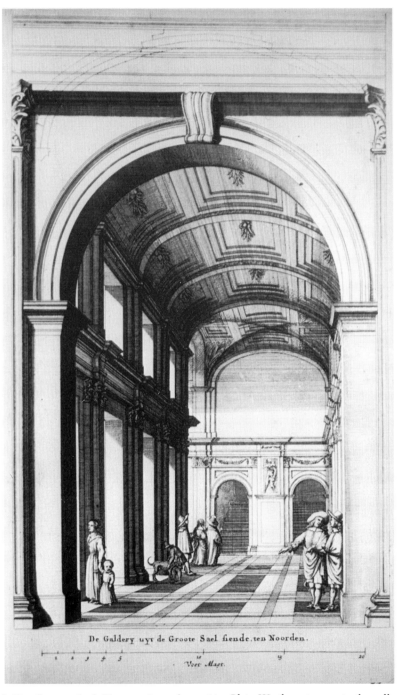

De Galdery uyt de Groote Sael ſiende, ten Noorden.

Voet Maet.

5. Jacob Van Campen *Stadt Huys van Amsterdam*, 1664, Plate W, the entrance to the gallery seen from the great hall.

6. Jacob Van Campen *Stadt Huys van Amsterdam*, 1664, Plate AQQ, panel of martial trophies.

7. Paul Decker, *Architectura Civilis*, 1711, Plate 55, sectional elevation of the Royal Chapel.

grandiose extensions of Hopetoun House beginning in 1721 cannot be said, even in their scale and sweep, to owe their inspiration to Decker. Adam can hardly have known the book at the time this work was planned yet, when he came to consider the internal arrangements at Arniston, about 1732, it seems clear that Decker's ideas were available to him. The front hall at Arniston (Fig. 8) has been explained as an attempt by Adam to catch the drama and movement of Vanbrugh's hall at Castle Howard.[22] There is no doubting that there are thematic similarities between the two rooms but the most striking feature of Adam's design is surely the use of high open arches, accommodated within the cover of the hall ceiling, which provide views from the first floor gallery back and down into the hall. This 'pierced-membrane' type of structure is commonplace in German Baroque architecture and just such a feature as these high arches was proposed for two of the principal rooms of Paul Decker's great Royal Palace: in fictive form in the Audience Chamber of the palace and as real open-arched galleries in the Chapel Royal (Fig. 7). In the chapel the lower section of the galleries was to be filled with a solid plinth in place of a balustrade, directly comparable to the solution that Adam adopted in Arniston hall. Here the application of the German pattern-book source to the front hall of an early Georgian country house is not perhaps quite as precise as the link between Francini's *Architecture* and the gateway to the Argyll Lodging or the mural monuments based on its title page, nevertheless, for once at least in William Adam's architecture, the nature and fact of his borrowing seems absolutely clear.

8. William Adam. The Entrance Hall of Arniston House, c. 1732.

In 1748 William Adam's library descended with Blair Adam itself to his eldest son, John. The more up-to-date volumes in the collection seem to reflect Robert Adam's attempts to keep his brother *à la page* for it must have been he who was responsible for adding Ferdinando Ruggieri, *Scielta di Architecture Antiche e Moderne di Firenze*, a monumental if dull four-volume reportage of Florentine buildings published in 1755, to the collection. He probably bought Pietro Ferrerio, *Palazzi di Roma*, and it was no doubt Bob who insisted that Blair Adam should have a complete set of Piranesi's *Antichità Romane* and the polemical *Della Magnificenza ed Architettura dei Romani*. William Adam seems to have owned a copy of Desgodetz's *Edifices Antiques de Rome*, a publication which Robert had wanted to purchase in London and to have sent to him in Rome because, as he wrote in June 1755, there was 'no such book to be found here for love nor money',[23] and it was no doubt he who procured J.D. Le Roy's *Ruines des Plus Beaux Monuments de la Grèce*, published in Paris in 1758, for his brother. John later purchased Stuart and Revett's *Antiquities of Athens*, which is noted in the catalogue 'no 2nd vol of this published yet'.

John's own great pleasure lay in gardening at North Merchiston and in the management of his estate at the Blair. The set of plans in his father's library of Stowe Park in Buckinghamshire would have complemented this interest which is also reflected in his own purchase of Edwards and Darly's *Chinese Designs* of 1754 and the handsome set of *Plans and Elevations of Kew* published by Sir William Chambers in 1763. These represent

21)

the design side of an interest that was also intensely practical, and we should note in closing this account that, besides these few new architectural volumes, John was to add no less than thirty-three titles on agriculture, husbandry and the practical aspects of gardening, all published within the second half of the century.[24]

APPENDIX

The following list of architectural books is taken from the full manuscript catalogue of the Library at Blair Adam, prepared in the late 1780s. The order and placing of volumes in the original catalogue is random reflecting the need to fit books of a certain size into particular shelves rather than any logical pattern of grouping by subject or interest area. The volumes are entered in the catalogue by shelf number with an approximate title followed by information on the size of the book, the number of volumes, the place and the year of publication: thus the entry for William Adam's copy of Serlio appears under Shelf No. 33 as 'Architetura di Sabastiano [sic] Serlio, Folio, 1, Paris, 1545' while the entry for the most modern architectural acquisition is given under Shelf No. 32 as 'Original Designs in Architecture, By Wm. Thomas, Folio, 1, London 1783'. In the present list the volumes are entered under the following headings: Editions of Vitruvius, Antiquities, Fortifications, Garden design, Architecture, Technical treatises and Books on art, topography and views. The lists are arranged alphabetically by author and in the Architecture section are further divided according to the country of origin. The brief titles, as given in the catalogue, are retained here with additions and editorial comments placed in square brackets. The use of capital letters in titles has been standardised.

EDITIONS OF VITRUVIUS

Vitruvius,* (1523)	[The date suggests the small volume published in Lyon and based on the Giunta Florentine edition of 1522 and the Como edition of 1521. The book's most remarkable feature is the quantity of Gothic plates, illustrating Book 4, including Notre Dame in Paris].
Vitruvius (Venice, 1567)	[*De Architectura Libri Decem.* A second printing of the 1556 edition by Daniele Barbaro and Palladio].
Vitruvio	[noted 'Italian wants the title page']
Perrault, Claude	*Architecture generale de Vitruve,* 'abrégé par Mr. Perrault', (Amsterdam, 1681). [Presumably a Dutch edition of Perrault's *Abrégé des dix livres d'architecture de Vitruve* (Paris, 1674): A little rule book intended to correct the confused ideas of Philibert de l'Orme whose abridgement up to then had been in use].
Perrault, Claude	*L'Architecture de Vitruve,* (Paris, 1734).

ANTIQUITIES

Adam, Robert	*Ruins of* [*the palace of the Emperor Diocletian at*] *Spalatro*, (London, 1764).
Barbault, [Jean]	[*Les Plus Beaux*] *Monuments de Rome Ancienne*, (Rome, [Bouchard & Gravier], 1761).
Bartoli, Pietro Santi	*Gli antiche sepolcri,* [*overo mausolei romani, et etruschi, trovati a Roma ed in altri luoghi celebri*], (Rome, 1697).
Bartoli, Pietro Santi	*Pictura Antiquacryptarum Romanorum*, (Rome, 1750).
Bartolus [Bartoli, P.S.]	*Antiquitatum Romanium.* [*Admiranda Romanarum antiquitatum ac veteris sculpturae vestigia anaglyphtico opere elaborata,* (Rome, Jo. Jacobus de Rubeis, 1685)].
Cavalleri, Gio. Battista	*Antiquam Statuarum Urbis Romae*, (1585).
Desgodetz, Antoine	*Les edifices antiques de Rome*, (Paris, 1682).
Donate, Alri	*Roma vetus ac recens illustrata*, (Amsterdam, 1694).
Fontana, Carlo	*L'Anfiteatro Flavio descritto e delineato*, (Haia, [I. Vaillant], 1725).
Le Roy, J[ulien].D[avid].	*Ruines des* [*plus beaux*] *monuments de la Grèce*, (Paris, 1758).
Montano, Gio. Battista*	*Architectura.* [Montano's work, often bound into one volume, consists in its most extended form of five titles: *Scielta d. varii tempietti antichi; libro primo & litro secondo* (Rome, G.B. Soria, 1624–1625); *Diversi ornamenti cavati dall' antico*, (Rome, Calisto Ferrante, 1636); *Diversi ornamenti capricciosi per depositi o altari*, (Rome, 1625); *Tabernacoli diversi nouamente unventati*, (Rome, G.B. Sonia, 1628); *Raccolta de tempii, et sepolcri disegnati dall antico*, (Rome, Calisto Ferrante, 1638) Editions vary greatly and there is no indication as to how many of these different titles were in the volume entitled 'Architectura' at Blair Adam].
Piranesi, Gio. Battista	*Le Antichità Romane*, 4 Vols, (Rome, [1756–1757]).
Piranesi, Gio. Battista	*Della magnificenza ed architettura dei Romani*, [Rome, 1764].
Stuart, James & Revett, N[icholas]	The antiquities of Athens, (London, 1762)[Noted 'no 2nd vol of this published yet'].
Wood, Robert	*Ruins of Palmyra*, (London, 1753).
Wood, Robert	*Ruins of Balbec*, (London, 1757).
No author	*A book of ancient figures and statues*, (London).

FORTIFICATION

Alghisi da Carpe, M. Galasso	*Delle fortificationi*, [*libri tre*, (Venice, 1570)].
Muller, John*	[Treatise containing the elementary part of] *Fortification*, (London, 1746).
Savary, T.	*Kochoorn's Fortification*, (London, 1705).
De Cambray, Chevalier	*Maniere de fortifier de M. de Vauban*, (Amsterdam, 1689).
De Ville, Antoine	*Les fortifications, attaques & defences de places*.
No author	Maps, plans of fortifications, battles &c.

GARDEN DESIGN

Chambers, [Sir] William	*Plans, elevations,* [*sections and perspective views of the gardens and buildings*] *at Kew* [*in Surrey*], (London, 1763).
Dezallier D'Argenville, Antoine Joseph*	*La théorie & la practique de jardinage*, (Paris, 1713).
Félibien, André	*Description de la grotte de Versailles*, (Paris, 1769).
No author	*Stowe, Description, plan, views etc.*

ARCHITECTURE: ITALIAN TITLES

Bartoli, Pietro Santi	*Disegno della loggia de San Pietro in Vaticano*, (Rome, 1684).
Brunetti, Gaetano	*see* Architecture: English titles.
Falda, Giovanni Battista	*Architetura* [*Il nuovo teatro delle fabriche et edificii, in prospettiva di Roma moderna, sotto il felice pontificato di N.S. Papa Alessandro VII*, (Roma, G.J. Rossi, 3 Vols, 1665–c. 1670). Only two volumes are listed in the catalogue].
Ferrerio, Pietro	*Palazzi di Roma* [*de più celebri architetti,* – (Rome, G.J. Rossi, c. 1675).
Guarini, Guarino	*Architetura Civile*, (Torino, [G. Mairesse], 1737).
Montani, Gio. Battista	*Architetura* [*see* Antiquities *above*].
Palladio, Andrea	*Architetura,* [*I quattro libri dell'Architettura di Andrea Palladio*] (Venice, [Bart. Carampello], 1581).
Pozzo, Andrea	*see* Architecture: English titles.
Ruggieri, Ferdinando	*Scielta di Architeture Antiche e Moderne* [*della Citta*] *di Firenze*, 4 Vols, (Firenze, 1755).
Rusconi, Gio. Antonio	*Architetura,* [*Della Architettura, libri dieci*](Venice, 1660). A

second enlarged edition of Rusconi's practical synthesis of Vitruvius, published in 1590.

Scamozzi, Vincenzo	*Architetura, [L'Idea della architettura universale]*(Venice, 1615).
Serlio, Sebastiano	*Architetura, [Il primo (secondo-quinto) libro d'architettura, mis en langue fr. par J. Martin]* (Paris, 1545).
No author	*Novum Theatrum Pedemontii et Sabaudii* (Hago Com, 1726).
No author	'Buildings of Venice, Etc.'

ARCHITECTURE: FRENCH TITLES

Bosse, A.	*Traité &c de l'Architecture Antique. [Traité des Manières de Dessiner Les Ordres de L'Architecture Antique en toutes leur parties]*(Paris, [1664]).
Cordemoy, Mons [J.L.] de	*[Nouveau traité de toute l'] Architecture, [ou l'art de bastir]*, (Paris, 1714).
Daviler, Le Sr. [A.C.]	*Cours d'Architecture qui comprend les Ordres de Vignole*, 2 vols. (Paris, [J. Mariette], 1694).
Daviler, Le Sr. [A.C.]	*Architecture*, (Paris, 1710)[marked 'vol 1 but seems complete'. This volume is either Daviler's edition of *Scamozzi* or the second edition of the *Cours*, also published in 1710].
Davilier, Le Sr. [A.C.]	*Architecture*, (Paris, 1738), [marked 'seems the same but a larger copy].
De L'Orme, Philibert	*[Nouvelles]Inventions pour Bien Bastir [et à petits fraiz]*, (Paris, 1561).
De L'Orme, Philibert	*Oeuvres, [Le premier tôme de l'Architecture]*, (Paris, [3rd edition also containing the *Nouvelles Inventions]*, 1626).
Du Cerceau, J[acques] A[ndrouet]	*[Le premier (-second) volume des plus excellents] Bastiments de France*, (Paris, 1607). [A reissue of the original editions of 1576 and 1579].
Du Cerceau, [J.A.]	*[Livre d'] Architecture [des plus excellents bastimens de France,]*(Paris, [the last reissue of Du Cerceau's original plates], 1648).
Félibien [André, Sieur des Avaux],	*[Des]Principles de l'Architecture et de la Sculpture [de la peinture, et des autres arts qui en dependent. Avec un dictionnaire des termes]*, (Paris, [3rd edition], 1697).
[Freart, Roland]	*Parallèle de l'architecture antique et de la moderne*, (Paris

	[Pierre Emery] 1702)
	see also Architecture: English titles.
La Joue, Le Sr.	*Recueil Nouveau de differens Cartouche*, (Paris).
Laugier, Marc Antione	*Essai sur l'Architecture*, (Paris, [Duchesne], 1755).
Le Clerc, Sébastien	*see* Architecture: English titles.
Le Muet, Pierre	*Manièr de Bastir*[*pour toutes sortes de personnes*], (Paris, [3rd edition], 1681).
Le Pautre, Antoine	[*Les Oeuvres d'*]*Achitecture* [*d'Antoine Le Pautre*], (Paris, 1652). [A set of plates of the 'Discours Cinquième' illustrating the *Hôtel de Mons. le Marquis de Fontenay Marville* is listed separately].
Mariot	*Architecture de Mariot.* [Probably Daniel Marot, *Oeuvres* (La Haye, 1703)].
Marot, Jean	*Recueil de plans & des palais & c, dans Paris.* [*Recueil des Plans, profils et elevations Des plusieurs palais. Chasteaux, Eglises, Sculptures, Grotes et Hostels, Batis dans Paris et aux environs.* This is the 'Petit Marot' of *c.*1665].
Meissonnier, J.A.	*Oeuvre de Juste Aurèle Meissonnier*, (Paris, *c.*1750).
No author	*Description General de l'Hôtel Royal des Invalides*, (Paris, 1683).
No author	'French buildings, views towns, prints & c'.
No author	*Histoire de l'Hôtel Royal des Invalides*, (Paris, 1736).
No author	*Plans, profils &c de ville et chateau de Versailles &c*, (Paris, 1715).
No author	*Architecture Historique* Dutch & French, (Paris, 1721).
No author	'French Chimneys, Sections &c' [Possibly a second copy of C.L. Genneté *Nouvelles constructions see* Foreign technical treatises *below*].

ARCHITECTURE: DUTCH AND GERMAN TITLES

Campen, Jacob van	[*Afbeelding van't*]*Stadt Huys Van Amsterdam*, (Amsterdam, 1664 [or 1668?]).
Decker, Paul	[*Furstlicher Baumeister, oder:*]*Architectura Civilis*, (Augsburg, 1711 [part ii, 1713 and part iii 1716]).
Guernery, Joa[chim?] Fra[ncis]	*Delineatio Montis Hess: Cass & c*, (Casselles, 1706).

Sturmis, Goldmannis & Leo Christian	*Prodromus Archit.*, (Augsburg, 1714).

ARCHITECTURE: ENGLISH TITLES

Brunetti, Gaetano*	*Sixty different sorts of Ornaments*, (London, 1736).
Campbell, Colen	*Vitruvius Britannicus*, 3 vols, (London, 1725).
Castell, Robert	[The] *Villas of the Ancients* [illustrated], (London, 1728).
Chambers, [Sir] William	[A treatise on the decorative part of civil] *Architecture*, (London, 1751).
Chippendale, Thomas	*The gentleman and cabinet maker's director*, (London, 1754).
Dugdale, Sir William	[A] *History of St. Paul's Cathedral*, (London, 1716).
Edwards and Darly,	*Chinese designs*, (London, 1754).
Fréart, Roland	*Parallel of ancient and modern architecture*, (London, 1733). Marked 'from the Frence'.
Garret, Daniel	*Designs and estimates of farmhouses*, (London, 1747).
Gibbs, James	*A book of architecture*, (London, 1728).
Gibbs, James	*Rules for drawing the several parts of Architecture* (London, 1738).
Gibbs, James	*Description of the Radcliffe Library, Oxford*, (London, 1747).
Jones, William	*The Gentleman or Builders' Companion* [containing a variety of useful designs for doors, gateways, peers, pavilions, temples, chimney-pieces etc.](London, 1739). Two copies.
Kent, William	*Designs of Inigo Jones*, [with some additional designs], (London, 1727).
Kirby, [John] Joshua	[The]*Perspective of Architecture*, [deduced from the principles of Dr. Brooke Taylor], (London, 1761).
Langley, Batty	*Gothic architecture* (London, 1742). [The catalogue here uses the common title for Langley's work: the proper title for the 1742 edition is *Ancient Architecture Restored and Improved*].
Langley, Batty	*Young builder's rudiments*, [or the principles of geometry, mechanics etc geometrically demonstrated,] (London, 1730).
Le Clerc, Sébastien	[*Traité d'*]*Architecture*, [noted 'translated by Chambers' (London). Le Clerc's treatise was published in Paris in 1714. The full title of Chambers's English edition is *A Treatise of architecture with remarks and observations necessary for young people who would apply themselves to that noble art*, 2 parts, (London, John Sturt, 1723)].

Leoni, Giacomo   *Palladio's Architecture*, [*The architecture of A. Palladio, revised, designed and published by Giacomo Leoni*], 3 vols, (London, 1715).

Leoni, Giacomo   *The architecture of L.B. Alberti*, 3 vols, (London, 1726).

Leyburn, William*   *The Mirror of Architecture*, (London, 1734). [This is the 7th edition of the English version of Scamozzi's *Architectural universale* (*see* above) edited by William Fisher. A section entitled 'Architectonia' by Leybum was added in 1700].

Oakley, Edward   [*The magazine of*] *architecture, perspective and sculpture*, (Westminster, 1730).

Pain, William   *The builder's companion* [*and workman's general assistant*], (London, 1758).

Price, Francis   [*The*]*British carpenter*, [*or a treatise on carpentry*](London, 1735).

Pozzo, Andrea   *Perspective for painters and architects*, (London, J. Sturt, 1747).

Salmon, William   *Architecture*, [perhaps *Palladio Londinensis* as the date given is 1734].

Salmon, William*   [The] *Builders' Guide and Gentleman and Traders' assistant; [or a universal] magazine of tables*, (London, 1736).

Salmon, William*   [The London and Country Builder's] *Vade mecum or [the compleat and universal] architect's assistant*, (London, 1745).

Thomas, William   *Original designs in architecture*, (London, 1783).

Vardy, John   *Some designs of Mr. Inigo Jones and Mr. William Kent*, (London, 1744). Two copies.

Ware, Isaac   *Plans, elevations etc. of Haughton*, (London, 1735).

Webb, John   [*A vindication of*] *Stonehenge* [*restored*], (London, 1665).

Wood, John   [*The*] *Origin of building*, [*or the plagarism of the heathens detected*], (Bath, 1741).

Wren, Sir Christopher*   *Designs for churches etc.*, [*Synopsis Aedificiorum Publicorum Dni Christophori Wren; A catalogue of the churches of the city of London*] (London, 1718).

FOREIGN TECHNICAL TREATISES

Agricola, Georgius   *De re mettallica, libri 12*, (Bas[ileae]Hel[vet], 1621).

Bélidor, [Bernard Forest de]   *Architecture Hydraulique, [ou l'art de conduire, d'elever et de menager les eaux pour les differens besoins de la vie]*, 2 Vols, (Paris, 1753).

Bion, N[icholas]	*Traité [de la construction et des principaux usages] des instrumens de mathematique,* (Haye, 1724).
Boecler [Johann Heinrich]	*Theatrum machinarum,* [marked 'wants 1st vol'].
Bosse, A[braham]	*Manière de graver a l'eauforte en cuivre,* (Paris, 1625).
Derand, R.P. Francois	*L'Architecture des voutes [ou l'art des traits et coupe des voutes],* (Paris, [Sebastien Cramoisy], 1643).
Desargues [Bosse, Abraham]	*La pratique du trait à preuves, de Mr. Desargues pour la coupe des pierres en l'architecture,* (1643).
Frezier,	*Traité de Stereotomie ou la coupe des pierres et du bois,* 3 vols, (Strassbourg, 1731).
Gallon, M.	*Recueil des machines approuvées par l'Academie Royal,* 6 vols, (Paris, 1735).
Genneté, Claude Léopold	*[Nouvelle] construction de cheminée qui garantit du feu & de la fumée,* (Liège, [F.J. Desoer], 1760).
Hulsius, Levinus	*Tractatus Instrumentem Mechanicorum,* (Frankfurt, 1605).
Morland, Le Chevalier	*Élévation des Eaux par toutes sortes de machines* (Paris, 1695).
No author	*L'Art de bâtir les vaisseaux, tirés des auteurs Hollandais,* (Amsterdam, 1719).
No author	*Theatrum machinarum universale,* 2 vols, (Amsterdam, 1736) [c.f. Boecleri *above*].

ART, TOPOGRAPHY, VIEWS ETC

Bloemaert, Abraham	*Forest des Hermites & Hermitesses d'Egypte et de la Palestine,* (Antwerp, 1619). [Seemingly an edition in French of Bloemaert's *Sylva anachoretica Aegypti et Palaestinae*; a charming volume with engraved pictures and brief lives of 50 saints].
Gibson, [Edmund]	*Camden's Britannia,* [The second edition of Bishop Gibson's translation], 2 vols, (London, 1722).
Lairesse, Gerard de	*The art of painting,* [noted 'translated by J.F. Fritsch'], (London, 1738).
Marolles, M. de	*Tableau du temple des muses,* (Amsterdam, 1674).
Parsons, Col. [William]	*A [New] Book of cyphers,* (Carlisle, 1703).
Piazzetta, Gian. Battista	*Studii di Pittura,* (Venice, 1760).
Picart le Romain,	*Images des heros, par J. Ange Cannini, gravées par Picart le*

Bernard	*Romain &c*, (Amsterdam, 1731).
Picart le Romain, B.	*Ovid's metamorphoses*, [noted 'Latin and English with cuts'], (Amsterdam, 1732).
Picart le Romain, B.	*The temple of the Muses*, (Amsterdam, 1733).
Picart le Romain, B.	*Ceremonies and religious customs of the various nations of the known world with plates* (London, 1733).
Richardson, [Jonathan] Sen. & Jr.	*Statues of Italy*, [An account of the statues and tax-reliefs, drawings and pictures in Italy, France etc.] (London, 1722).
[Sletzer, John]	*Theatrum Scotiae*, (London, [3rd Ed.] 1718).
[Speed, John]	*Theatre de la Grande Bretagne*, (London, 1724).
Turnbull, George	*A treatise on ancient painting*, (London, 1740).
William [W.]	*Oxonia Depicta*
No author	Effigies of painters and artists, (London, 1594).
No author	The Exchange of Edinburgh.
No author	*Persepolis Illustrata*, (London, 1739).
No author	*Practice of perspective by a Jesuit of Paris*, (London, 1749).
No author	*Sacred geography illustrated*, (London).
No author	Views, elevations etc., English, Dutch etc,

DRAWINGS

The catalogue lists a number of volumes of drawings as follows: A large drawing book; A book of drawings, architecture, ornaments &c; A portfolio containing plans etc of a house; A portfolio containing plans and sections of a Bagnio; Plans of houses, gardens, pictures &c, &c.; Landscapes, etc. by several hands.

*In the time available to me it has not been possible to identify all titles fully: some may not be difficult. I am grateful to Dr. Eileen Harris for the amplification of the titles marked with an asterisk.

NOTES

1. Ian Mowat, 'An eighteenth-century private library: The books of William and John Adam at Blair Adam', *The Library Review*, Vol. 8, Spring 1979. The *Catalogue of the Blair Adam Library*, was printed by Clowes & Sons, London, in 1883.

2. I am grateful to Keith Adam for drawing my attention to this document, discovered at Blair Adam in 1988, and for his kindness in letting me have a copy of the architectural entries.

3. One manuscript volume of designs, apparently by William Adam, and

bearing John Adam's bookplate was sold at Sothebys in June 1981 and is now in the collection of the Victoria and Albert Museum (photographs of the drawings are in the National Monuments Record for Scotland). The thirty-five pages contain thirty-nine drawings of the plans and elevations of a three-storey, nine-bay house (with side elevations reminiscent of Arniston) together with a variety of gate piers, urns, finials, enriched mouldings drawn large, balusters, scrollwork, carved panels and borders, chimney breasts and the interior elevations of a panelled room. This volume does not relate precisely to any of the descriptions in the manuscript library catalogue. The whereabouts of the other material is unknown. I am grateful to Ian Gow for drawing my attention to this volume.

4. John Summerson, *Architecture in Britain 1530–1830*, 3rd Ed. 1958, p. 317. An earlier case of continental influence on the classical architecture of Scotland may be the doorcase of the Chapel Royal at Stirling castle building from 1594 which is apparently based on the frontispiece of Perret's design. Deborah Howard points out however that both designs derive in essence from the Arsenal Gateway in Venice.

5. These Italian pattern-book sources for Heriot's Hospital are illustrated in *Country Life*, 6 March 1975, pp. 554 & 557.

6. Alexandre Francine, *Livre D'Architecture contenant Plusieurs Portiques de Differentes Inventions* (Paris, 1631).

7. The Mylne monument was erected in memory of John Mylne, died 1667. It is described in the Royal Commission on the Ancient Monuments of Scotland, *The City of Edinburgh* (Edinburgh; H.M.S.O., 1951), p. 68 and illustrated as Fig. 206. See also Robert Scott Mylne, *The Master Masons to the Crown of Scotland* (Edinburgh, 1893), p. 160.

8. A third version of the Francini title page adapted as a mural monument occurs in the monument to Bishop George Wishart, died 1671, in the North aisle of Holyrood Abbey, Edinburgh. This monument is described but not illustrated in the Royal Commission, *The City of Edinburgh* (H.M.S.O., 1951), p. 139.

9. The Argyll Lodging is described and illustrated in the Royal Commission on the Ancient Monuments of Scotland, Stirling, (Edinburgh, H.M.S.O., 1963, p. 277–84.

10. As Dugdale's History also illustrated much of the medieval architecture of old St Pauls, the book was frequently used in the early eighteenth century as a source book for Gothic designs. It is interesting to note the occurrence of Dugdale in the Blair Adam catalogue as John, Robert and James Adam all dabbled in a form of evocative Rococo Gothic architecture in their early careers.

11. The fourth copy of Vitruvius appears in the manuscript catalogue as 'Vitruvio, Italian wants the title page'. The library also contained a Dutch edition (Amsterdam, 1681) of Perrault's abridgement of Vitruvius, *Architecture General de Vitruve* first published in Paris in 1674.

12. Rusconi, *Della architettura*, Venice 1590.

13. Christopher Wren, *Parentalia, or Memoirs of the Family of Wren*, (London, 1750. Ed. by Ernest J. Enthoven, 1903, p. 106.

14. For Lord Milton's volumes *see below*. It is possible that a number of the continental titles did not find their way into the Blair Adam library until after William Adam's death, and that they were purchased in a regular way by Robert or James while abroad. We cannot tell how far the younger brother behaved like bibliographic magpies while abroad though it may be worth noting that they tended to buy *for themselves* with an eye to their London practice and it seems unlikely that the exotic material from the seventeenth century and Baroque periods would have been passed on to John Adam in Edinburgh. Key modern works, like J.D. Le Roy on Greek architecture or some of the volumes by Piranesi were clearly in a different category.

15. It seems more probable that Robert Adam would have been attracted to purchase Montano's manuscript having already known the book than that he would have purchased both the book and the manuscript while abroad.

16. It is tempting to suggest that Sir James Clerk of Penicuik (or the younger John Baxter) may also have owned a copy of Montano's designs as the title page to one part, *Raccolta de Tempii e sepolcri desegnati dall' Antico*, shows a doorway flanked by loosely-clad Druidical figures, very similar to those that were carved by Willie Jeans in 1776 for the niches on either side of the front door of the house. See *Country Life*, 15 August 1968, p. 384, Pl. 4 & 5.

17. National Library of Scotland, MS. 16580, f. 3. William Adam to Andrew Fletcher, Lord Milton, 13 March 1740. Quoted by Ian Mowat, *Op. Cit.*

18. William Adam, *Vitruvius Scoticus* (reprinted by Paul Harris, Edinburgh, 1980), p. 30 and Pl. 45.

19. It is noteworthy how many of the architectural titles, listed in the Blair Adam catalogue, recurred in James Gibbs's library. These parallels and the range and modernity of the collection built up by Adam largely contradicts the notion of his having been no more than an interesting provincial designer.

20. Van Campen's use of this motif is seen particularly in the arched screens that open into the galleries on either side and at either end of the great central hall (Plate W in the *Stadthuys*). Examples in Adam's architecture occur in the hall of The Drum, Gilmerton, the hall at Arniston, Midlothian, and in the Saloon at the House of Dun, Angus. The entrance hall at Hopetoun was also to have been remodelled in this way.

21. For Newliston see A.T. Bolton, *The Architecture of Robert and James Adam* (London, Country Life, 1922), Vol. II, p. 278–87.

22. This case is argued by John Fleming in *Robert Adam and His Circle in Edinburgh and Rome* (London, John Murray, 1962), pp. 68–9.

23. *Ibid.*, p. 171.

24. John Adam was perhaps also interested in perspective: the library held four volumes on this topic three of which might well have been bought by him. The volumes on perspective were Edward Oakley, *Architecture, Perspective and Sculpture* (Westminster, 1730); Andrea Pozzo, *Perspective for Painters and Architects* (London, J. Strut, 1747); no author, *The Practice of Perspective by a Jesuit of Paris* (London, 1749) and Joshua Kirby, *Perspective of Architecture* (London, 1761).

This article discusses the architectural contents of the library at Blair Adam and the books which William Adam will have used in the evolution of his own designs. The range of over 140 titles from Italy, France, Germany, the Netherlands and Britain illustrates clearly both the seriousness of Adam's purpose and the modernity of his ideas. Far from being a mere provincial collection the library was the creation of a cosmopolitan connoisseur.

This article discusses the architectural contents of the library at Blair Adam and the books which William Adam will have used in the evolution of his own designs. The range of over 140 titles from Italy, France, Germany, the Netherlands and Britain illustrates clearly both the seriousness of Adam's purpose and the modernity of his ideas. Far from being a mere provincial collection the library was the creation of a cosmopolitan connoisseur.

'Mr *Inigo Pilaster* and Sir *Christopher Cupolo*': On the Advantages of an Architectural Farrago

The intention behind the rather outlandish title of this paper is to suggest how the remarkable achievement of William Adam, perhaps the only eighteenth-century Scottish architect practising at home who succeeded in producing a substantial body of highly individual work of more than parochial interest (though this achievement has rarely been seen as belonging to the wider arena of British architecture), accorded with ideas and fashions south of the border, where many of the most important early Georgian architectural innovations were being made.[1]

PROBABLY the outstanding event of this period was the appearance in London in 1715 of Colen Campbell's illustrated book *Vitruvius Britannicus*, a miscellany of mainly domestic buildings dating from the early seventeenth to the early eighteenth centuries, bolstered by a brief but persuasive introduction defending the classical tradition of the Italian Renaissance by ridiculing the Baroque buffooneries of Bernini and his followers. Campbell praised the architects of the fifteenth and sixteenth centuries, above all Andrea Palladio, as the '*Restorers of* Architecture [who] *have greatly help'd to raise this Noble Art from the Ruins of Barbarity*' (that is, from the Gothic past), and he contrasted their great achievement with the work of modern Italian architects who '*can no more now relish the Antique Simplicity, but are entirely employed in capricious Ornaments*', offering as examples the '*affected and licentious. . .Works of* Bernini *and* [Carlo] Fontana' and the '*wildly Extravagant. . .Designs of* Boromoni, *who has endeavoured to debauch Mankind with his odd and chimerical Beauties*'. Campbell demonstrated his premise by devoting the inaugural illustrations to a criticism of the early seventeenth-century Baroque additions made by Bernini and Carlo Maderno to St Peter's in Rome: not only did he condemn the 'trifling. . .Breaks', 'mean' pediment and 'excessive Height of the *Attick*', but believed that the 'Parts [are] without Proportion' and that the extended nave 'extremely injured the August Appearance of [Michelangelo's] Cupola'. These absurdities were then sharply contrasted with Campbell's own '*new Design for a Church in* Lincolns-Inn Fields' (1712, unbuilt) which possessed 'a regular Hexastyle [portico and was] dress'd very plain, as most conformable to the Simplicity of the Ancients'. Inigo Jones's 'incomparable' Banqueting House at Whitehall (1619–22) was offered as an examplar of 'Strength with Politeness, Ornament with Simplicity, Beauty with Majesty', while William Benson's recently completed Wilbury House (1710) is described as a 'beautiful and regular Design. . .in the Stile of *Inigo Jones*' and Campbell's own design of 1715 for Lord

Perceval, based on Palladio's villas, was commended for omitting 'all manner of Rusticks and other Ornaments generally practised, purely to shew the Harmony of Proportion in the greatest Simplicity'.[2] In this way, the first volume of *Vitruvius Britannicus* (and the two subsequent volumes, published in 1717 and 1725) succeeded in implanting in the minds of Campbell's contemporaries the politically appealing, though aesthetically untenable, notion that the purity of the preferred style was superior to the hybrid one of the other; and, furthermore, that henceforth this new classicism was to be regarded as the sole and unquestioned rule of national taste, with Palladio, Jones, Campbell and Richard Boyle, the third Earl of Burlington, presiding as its chief arbiters.

In the frontispiece of Giacomo Leoni's magnificent English edition of *The Four Books of Architecture*, published in London in 1716, the Order of the Garter sheds golden beams of light on an heroic bust of Palladio.[3] In William Kent's *The Designs of Inigo Jones*, published in 1727, the work of Palladio and his English follower are linked as 'equal Proofs of the Superiority of those two Great Masters to all others', and in *An Essay In Defence of Ancient Architecture*, 1728, Robert Morris lauds 'that great Architect *Andrea Palladio*' and speaks of a time 'in our own Country in the Last Century, when the rude *Gothick* way began to be despis'd, and true Architecture flourish'd under the Conduct of INIGO JONES'.[4] In *The Art of Architecture: A Poem In Imitation of Horace's Art of Poetry*, 1742, Morris offered this advice:

> Few are the Ornaments, but plain and neat,
> The *least* REDUNDANT are the *most* COMPLEAT.
> Learn of PALLADIO, how to deck a Space;
> Of JONES you'll learn Magnificence, and Grace:
> CAMPBELL will teach, the Beauty they impart;
> And GIBBS, the Rules and Modus of the Art:
> Keep still these Rules, and Methods, in your Sight;
> Read them by Day, and Meditate by Night.[5]

So insistently did this clique preach its message that generations of architects, builders and their clients, not to mention critics and historians, (even up to our own time) have come to accept *Palladian* classicism as the only legitimate style (except for gothic) which could, and indeed was, practised during the early Georgian period. In his survey of the years between 1715 and 1750 in *Architecture in Britain*, John Summerson illustrated almost no buildings which wandered from this ideology, concentrating instead on the master-pieces of Lord Burlington, identified as the High Priest of Palladianism, and his devout congregation–Campbell, Flitcroft, Kent, Leoni, Roger Morris, the Earl of Pembroke, Wood of Bath. The Aberdonian James Gibbs (who was a Catholic and had trained in Rome under Carlo Fontana, the Papal Architect) is given a separate chapter because of 'his inaccessibility to the more doctrinaire influences of his time', while the buildings of Gibbs's contemporary and fellow-countryman, William Adam, are summarily dis-missed because they 'reflect the mixed influence of Wren, the Palladians, and Gibbs

[with] no desire to discriminate between them'.[6] Such a lopsided view of the British architectural scene in the early eighteenth century excludes entire regiments of worthy metropolitan and provincial practitioners who represented an impressive and stubborn opposition to the Pantheon of Palladian 'Greats'. Moreover, by far the majority of buildings of any pretence put up during the thirty-five or forty years following the appearance of the first volume of *Vitruvius Britannicus* in 1715 did not subscribe to its dogma, but rather followed an 'alternative' approach, a sort of architectural farrago out of which a talented man might brew a distinctive and winning way of working.[7]

Alexander Pope hinted at such a hybrid approach in a poem dating exacty contemporary with Campbell's revolutionary 1715 manifesto. 'The Temple of Fame' describes a fictitious building composed of a sumptuous west front with 'Doric pillars of white marble [and an] architrave of antique mold', an 'East front [with] diamond flaming, and Barbaric gold',

> on the south, a long majestic race
> Of Aegypt's Priests the gilded niches grace

and finally,

> Of Gothic structure was the northern side,
> O'erwrought with ornaments of barb'rous pride.[8]

With the arrival in the 1730s of widespread popular journalism the subject of stylistic appropriateness in architecture received frequent and often acrimonious airings. Characteristic is the article originally published in *The Universal Spectator* (No. 190, 27 May 1732) and reprinted in the May 1732 issue of *The Gentleman's Magazine*, a fashionable monthly journal of literature, news and gossip, entitled '*Of Extravagance in Building*'. This relates how Jenny Downcastle gives Mr Stonecastle 'her Thoughts on Modern Architecture, and defies him to produce in all his Inventory of female Extravagancies any Thing so enormous, so expensive, so exposing as your modern Vanity of *Buildings*', for 'All these fall among your own Sex; you have no *Vitruvius*, no *Palladio* in Petticoats'! She then lampoons those '*designing Virtuosi* who have signaliz'd themselves for this *Grand Gusto* of distorting and disguising the Face of Nature, [and who] have qualified me to characterize the most conspicuous of them, from their renown'd Examplars Mr *Inigo Pilaster* and Sir *Christopher Cupolo*'. 'Mr Alderman *Pantiles* [and] Mr *Afterthought* his *Undertaker*' (that is, his architect) are attacked for spending £1000 a year building 'a *Quarry* above Ground', while his 'darling Son has been rambling about *Italy* to refine his Taste in Building' and his 'only Daughter [is] denied every Accompolishment, because her Shape, forsooth, inclines to the *Tuscan*'! Finally, Miss Downcastle asks: 'Does not such gross and superficial Grandeur argue a Consciousness of intrinsick Littleness in the Master?. . .- Besides, shou'd his Varieties in Building be faulty in any of the numberless Niceties of Style, Symmetry or Situation, his Judgment must suffer as well as his Purse [for whereas]

A Miscarriage in Behaviour grows invisible in succeeding Acts. . .an architectural Blunder is a monumental Folly, always in Sight'.[9]

Architectural historians have tended to dismiss this sort of popular reportage as mere Georgian foppishness. While it is true that Jenny's diatribe is undeniably witty, as it was chiefly intended to be, there is also an underlying sense of entreaty from a bewildered public struggling to come to grips with the subtleties of architectural discourse. This seems to me to have been the condition in which Scottish architecture found itself during the years between 1720 and 1750 when the senior Adam served as its presiding genius.

William must certainly have been aware of some of these architectural discussions and controversies. In 1727, at the age of thirty-eight and with little more than a handful of houses to his credit (but including Mavisbank, Hopetoun, The Drum and Arniston), he made a momentous journey into England in company with the amateur architect, Sir John Clerk of Penicuik. From Clerk's manuscript diary we know they visited Cliveden, the earl of Orkney's Buckinghamshire estate, which Sir John disliked because of the 'vast expense. . .Laid out without taste or judgement'; the Caroline mansion remodelled around 1710 by Thomas Archer 'consists of various parts irregularly put together as his Lord's fancy or occasion requir'd'. On the other hand, Clerk was clearly smitten by Palladian virtues: he wrote enthusiastically of the mid-seventeenth century Jonesian remodelling of Wilton in Wiltshire, particularly of the 'very noble & gracefull' Double Cube Room; he also admired the nearby mansion at Amesbury (c. 1667) by Jones's pupil, John Webb, and regarded Campbell's recently completed country house at Wanstead in Essex as 'one of the best in England', commending especially the saloon as 'a fine Room well finish'd in Stuco'. When Clerk visited Burlington's villa at Chiswick the Architect Earl gave him some designs for windows from his collection of 'several hundred drawings of paladio & Inigo Jones'.[10] It is interesting that Cliveden, Wilton, Amesbury, Wanstead and Chiswick are all illustrated in *Vitruvius Britannicus* and that Clerk thought it noteworthy to record this fact in his diary.[11] A large number of Scottish country house owners subscribed to the volumes and it would appear that its revolutionary message had permeated to the far North by the time Clerk and Adam set out on their tour in 1727.

Yet, it might be that a truer indication of Clerk's taste, and perhaps Adam's as well, is reflected in the comments on buildings by James Gibbs. In the previous year, 1726, in a book entitled *Itinerarium Septentrionale: or, A Journey Thro' most of the Counties of Scotland, And Those in the North of England*, Gibbs had been praised for his advocacy of 'the noble Rules of Symmetry and Proportion in Architecture' as practised by Palladio, Jones and 'our Modern Artists. . .after so many Centuries of Ignorance and Darkness'. The author, Alexander Gordon, was a friend of Clerk (the two men had visited Hadrian's Wall together in 1724) and in his book Gordon went on to observe that 'if this fine Humour for Architecture subsist in the Nation, and such Buildings as the great Artist Mr Gibbs has adorn'd London with, continues to be carried on, very few Cities in Europe

(Rome excepted) will contend with it for Magnificience'.[12] Not surprisingly, Clerk and Adam visited his two great London churches, St Mary-le-Strand and St Martin-in-the-Fields, as well as the 'octagon Room' built between 1716 and 1721 at Twickenham for James Johnston (a former Secretary of State for Scotland), which Clerk found 'finely finish'd within in Stuco-work & Gilding'. They also saw the greenhouse (c.1723) at nearby Whitton Place, the estate of Archibald Campbell, Earl of Islay (for whom Adam was later to work at Inveraray).[13] Archibald was the younger brother of John Campbell, Duke of Argyll and Greenwich, for whom Gibbs had recently built Sudbrook House (1715–19) on the Surrey side of the Thames at Petersham. Argyll was the dedicatee of Gibbs's A Book of Architecture, to which both Clerk and Adam subscribed. This publication, containing over four hundred engraved designs exclusively by the architect (as distinct from Campbell's presentation in Vitruvius Britannicus), first appeared in 1728 and immediately became a highly influential pattern book. Adam was to make great use of it throughout his career.

Sometimes his borrowings were direct and uncomplicated, as in the case of the temple proposed for Eglinton in Ayrshire, which is modelled on Gibbs's circular temple at Hackwood Park in Hampshire published as plate 72 in A Book of Architure.[14] But in Adam's more spectacularly individual compositions the mixture of sources is more varied and eccentric—what Robert Morris might have condemned as a 'wild Heap of inconsistent Things',[15] but which to my eye appear to possess a Scottish virility which is far more exciting than the frankly boring appropriations of predictably Palladian patterns which characterise much of Adam's later domestic work, where idiosyncrasy and wit have all but vanished.

By contrast, Mavisbank in Midlothian—a youthful collaboration (1722–c.1728, with the owner, Sir John Clerk) of exceptional charm—is an amalgamation of motifs derived from Campbell's 'New Design of my own Invention in the Style of Inigo Jones' (1714) for the Duke of Argyll published as plate 20 in the first volume of Vitruvius Britannicus, and perhaps Louis Le Vau's Hôtel de Bretonvilliers in Paris as published by Jean Marot in the 1650s.[16] It is indicative of the early eighteenth century that identification of historical styles was still so mercurial that when the English antiquarian, Roger Gale, visited Mavisbank in 1739 he found 'one of the most elegant [estates] I ever saw for situation, wood, and water' but mistakenly described the house as being 'in a true Palladio tast'.[17]

At Dun House, Angus, which was building around 1728,[18] the South Front is indebted to plate 37 in A Book of Architecture, a rather dour design for 'a Person of Quality in Somersetshire'.[19] When Adam turned to the North Front, however, something quite exceptional took place. The general tripartite organisation as well as such details as the quoined corners and the central recessed porch crowned by a raised cornice with balustrade and vases and flanked by solid-panelled parapets, were clearly inspired by

Sudbrook, itself still only a tentative Palladian design from Gibbs's early career.[20] Into this Adam injected the curious idea of a grand Ionic triumphal arch-like frontispiece with blind outer bays and a taller central round-arched recess. The main door in the form of a Venetian Window is an odd transposition of function with precedence in an unexecuted scheme by John Vanbrugh for Eastbury in Dorset (1716) illustrated in the second volume of *Vitruvius Britannicus*.[21] The Dun frontispiece itself comes from an earlier, rejected design for the house offered by the owner's kinsman, John Erskine, 11th Earl of Mar, made while he was in exile in Paris in 1723.[22] It is also possible that Adam might have seen a design by James Smith, an older Scottish contemporary, for an unidentified church façade incorporating this unusual feature.[23] Dun, therefore, would seem to be an aggregation of hybrid Late Baroque and Proto-Palladian ideas.

The questions that need to be asked are whether Adam's Dun composition is the result of random and capricious borrowings by an untutored backwoodsman stranded far from metropolitan good sense and good taste (as some historians would have us believe), or whether Adam's genius blossomed best when operating outside the conventions imposed by dogma, thereby permitting the sort of creative synthesis characterised by Dun, or Duff and The Drum and Mavisbank and the splendid hall at Arniston? If the latter is the case, as I would like to believe, in the absence of any substantial body of writing by Adam himself which might throw light on his approach to architectural design, what matter of evidence can be brought to bear for interpreting his buildings in this way? Was there, for example, an accepted and accessible alternative creed to strict Palladianism to which Adam might have confidently turned for both corroboration and inspiration?

As it happens, Adam's emergence on to the architectural scene in the 1720s and thirties coincided with an unprecedented rash of writings on architecture and architectural criticism, exemplified by the comments of Jenny Downcastle and Robert Morris. The following letter appeared on 23 March 1734 in the pages of a popular London newspaper, *The Grub-street Journal*: 'Sir. . .It is somewhat hard, that a noble-man or gentleman cannot lay out six or eight thousand pounds of his own upon a house for himself, and in laying it out, execute two or three of his own whims, (which thou' they may not be strictly agreeable to true taste, yet hit his own) but some critic must immediately stigmatize him in print for it'. The author, who signed himself Atticus, can be identified as that well-known Twickenham landscape-architect and prolific publisher of popular pattern books, Batty Langley. His letter was a prelude to a series of twenty-six articles, written under the pseudonym Hiram, which appeared in *The Grub-street Journal* during 1734–35 as a response to the recently published book entitled *A Critical Review of the Publick Buildings, Statues and Ornaments In, and about London and Westminster*, published in 1734 by James Ralph, the first book of its kind in British literature.

In the dedicatory essay Ralph established the philosophical tone of his thesis: 'At a time. . .when so much money is lavish'd in building, and too often with so little

pretence to beauty, or magnificence [and] few have a. . .talent of laying out their
fortunes with propriety. . .it could not be unreasonable to publish some hints on a
subject so frequently employ'd, and so seldom understood. . .Folly in building is one of
the most lasting reflections on a man's character, because 'tis not only universally known
in his own time, but is often perpetuated thro' many generations. It is incumbent,
therefore, on every man of quality and fortune, to weigh very seriously every undertaking of this nature, and not percipitate himself into an expense, that neither convenience,
or grandeur can justify'. Ralph exorted his readers to consult the models provided by
Burlington, to whom *A Critical Review* is dedicated, and which he identified with the ideal
of 'Simplicity. . .the ground-work of beauty, [where] the fewer parts a building is
composed of, if they are harmonized with elegance and proportion, the more beautiful
it appears'. We must assume that Langley did not subscribe to Ralph's thesis.[24]

These two widely-circulated opposing documents of the 1730s–Ralph's *Critical Review*
and Langley's *Grub-street* counter-attack–offer valuable insights into the dissentious
nature of architectural theory and practice at the time: what Ralph identified as the
oppositions between truth and beauty, elegance and knowledge on the one hand, and on
the other folly and affectation, falsehood and deformity; in short, between 'the moderns
and the antediluvians'.[25] To take a few examples.

Langley berated Ralph for condemning Nicholas Hawksmoor's East End churches as
'mere Gothique heaps of stone, without form or order', citing Christ Church, Spital-
fields (1714–29) as 'beyond question, one of the most absurd piles in Europe'.[26] Langley
believed Hawksmoor's 'truely genuine designs [represented] a mean, between the Greek
and Gothique', and he pointed out that 'every judge of architecture, who has viewed and
examined those buildings. . .has always agreed, that their stiles and modes were truely
strong and magnificent, and at the same time light and genteel'.[27] Of course, Ralph was
using the term 'Gothique' not as a stylistic description but as an historical term of abuse,
meaning barbaric, just as Sir John Clerk had done in his 1727 poem, *The Country House*:
. . .on whom these Rules you waste,
For Goths will always have a Gothick taste.[28]
Langley, who believed that 'Porticos of large columns have a majestic aspect, and fill the
eye with solemn grandeur, when viewed at a proper distance',[29] attacked Thomas
Ripley's Admiralty in Whitehall (Fig. 1) completed 1726, as a 'tasteless and expensive'
progress towards architectural absurdity and failure, and singled-out the Ionic portico,
which 'gives a general distaste [because it is] too narrow a breadth for the whole front,
[the columns being] to high [and] their intercolumniation. . .much too small'. In a vain
attempt to rectify this 'lasting monument to the architect's ignorance [Ripley] increased
the heights of the shafts [of the columns] with. . .garden rolling stones', which Langley
'dignified. . .with the title of the Gruntic Order'.[30] With regard to William Kent's
Treasury Buildings in Whitehall (Fig. 2) under construction 1733–37, Ralph expressed

The Admiralty near White Hall.

1. The Admiralty, Whitehall, London, 1723–6, by Thomas Ripley (author's collection).

a hope that they would prove 'stately and august. . .grand and magnificent', all essential requisites of great public edifices.[31] But Langley was scandalised by the 'grotesque rustic arches of the lower storey', from which he concluded that 'magnificence in building doth not consist in enrichments only'.[32]

Both writers frequently commented on the treatment of cornices. Langley was appalled by Ralph's championship of the Whitehall Banqueting House and felt that though 'so much applauded for its supposed beauty, is really full of absurdities', among which he regarded as especially 'false' the many breaks in the entablature over the Order, comparing it unfavourably to the continuous entablature of Gibbs's St Martin-in-the-Fields (Fig. 3), which possesses a 'grandeur. . .according to the ancient manner'.[33] Langley also observed that entablatures 'should not be broken above columns [because they then] have more the aspect of a capital. . .and make the column seem to be crowded with capital super capital'.[34] He offered as more successful than Jones's hallowed solution George Sampson's new Bank of England (Fig. 4) 1732–35, describing the cornice (which Ralph regarded as 'rather too heavy for the building') as 'truely of proper dimensions [because the entablature has been] continued. . .throughout, in one part, [thereby achieving] a bold majestic projection'.[35] Finally, whereas Ralph applauded the steeple of St Martin's as 'one of the most tolerable in town', Langley thought it too low, affording

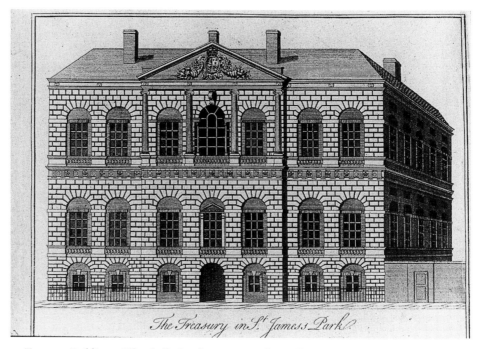

2. Treasury Buildings, Whitehall, London, 1733–7, by William Kent (author's collection).

'a most miserable poor appearance, much beneath that magnificency and grandeur which one would justly expect in the parish church of our sovereign lord the king', and he observed in regard to steeples generally that ' 'tis the loftiness and elegancy of buildings, that makes the views of cities magnificent'.[36]

Let us imagine William Adam cognisant of such debates, as he must surely have been, setting about designing Dundee Town House (Fig. 5).[37] This is one of his earliest civic enterprises (designed and built 1731–35, demolished 1932) and also one of his most interesting in that it reveals him struggling to establish a new public building type for Scotland using current architectural language yet turning to the form of the traditional Scottish tolbooth, with its tall tower. Heeding Langley's timely warnings, Adam applied to the main façade a dignified temple portico supporting a simple unbroken cornice, the whole raised on an arched basement of horizontal channelling carefully differentiated from the more condensed rustication of the main wall above. For this arrangement he most likely consulted a detail from plate 23 in Kent's *The Designs of Inigo Jones*, 1727 (Fig. 6), a scheme for a royal palace at Whitehall. In the case of the window detailing Adam and Langley would have parted ways. Sometimes referred to as a Gibbs-surround, though derived from Palladio's Palazzo Thiene at Vicenza, Langley abhorred this window form and campaigned rigorously for its elimination from the canon. He condemned the 'small block rustics' of Gibbs's steeple addition to St Clement Danes (1719) as being in a 'low

A Perspective View of St. Martins Church.

3. St Martin-in-the-Fields, London, 1720–6, by James Gibbs (Plate 1 in *A Book of Architecture*, 1728).

A Perspective View of the Bank of England.

4. Bank of England, London, 1732–5, by George Sampson (Plate III in *An Historical Catalogue of Engravings, Drawings and Paintings in the Bank of England*, 1928).

5. Dundee Town House, 1731–5, by William Adam (Plate 104 in *Vitruvius Scoticus*, 1812).

mince-pye taste', and at St Martin's breaking the window architrave with 'block rustics' interrupted the 'finest range of pillasters and columns yet erected, either by ancient or moderns [and] extreamly diminish[ed] the solemn grandeur' of the church.[38] Nevertheless, Adam amalgamated two alternative St Martin's designs in *A Book of Architecture*

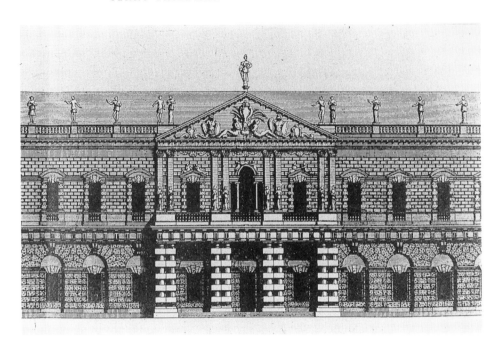

6. Project for Whitehall Palace, London (Plate 23, detail, in W. Kent, *The Designs of Inigo Jones*, 1727).

(plates 1 and 30) for the Dundee steeple. So, I suggest, Gibbs, Jones and Palladio, partly seen through Langley's and Ralph's eyes, became the models for Dundee; and typical of these farraginous times, Adam then added to this rich soup a range of oval windows which Langley would almost certainly have disliked, for he had condemned their use in other contemporary buildings on the grounds that they had 'the aspect of port-holes in a man of war'![39]

Leeds City Art Gallery and The Henry Moore Centre for the Study of Sculpture

NOTES

1. Information on architects and buildings mentioned in this essay can be found in H. Colvin, *A Biographical Dictionary of British Architects 1600–1840*, 1978. For Adam, see also J. Fleming, *Robert Adam and His Circle in Edinburgh & Rome*, 1962; J. Gifford, *William Adam 1689–1748: A Life and Times of Scotland's Universal Architect*, 1989; J. Macaulay, *The Classical Country House in Scotland 1660–1800*, 1987; J. Simpson, intro., *Vitruvius Scoticus William Adam*, 1980.

2. *Vitruvius Britannicus*, 1715, pp. 3, 5, 7, pls. 5–9, 12–3, 51–2, 95–7.

3. R. Wittkower, 'English Neoclassicism and the Vicissitudes of Palladio's "Quattro Libri" ', in *Palladio and English Palladianism*, 1974, p. 81, pl. 109.

46)

4. p. xii.

5. pp. 14, 25–6.

6. *Architecture in Britain*, 1970, pp. 347, 377. For a more recent interpretation of Gibbs's place in the eighteenth-century revival of classicism, see T. Friedman, *James Gibbs*, 1984.

7. See for example, John Erksine, 11th Earl of Mar's abortive designs for the Old Pretender's residence in Kensington, London (*Simpson*, p. 33, pl. 109–10; T. Friedman, 'A "Palace worthy of the Grandeur of the King": Lord Mar's designs for the Old Pretender, 1718–30', *Architectural History*, Vol. 29, 1986, pp. 102–19).

8. Lines 75–7, 93–4, 109–10, 119–20.

9. pp. 765–6.

10. Scottish Record Office: GD18/2107, 'journey to London in 1727', unnumbered pages.

11. *Vitruvius Britannicus*, 1715, p. 4, pls. 21–7; 1717, pp. 3–4, pls. 61–7, 70–4; 1725, pp. 7–8, pls. 7, 26, 39–40.

12. T. Friedman, *James Gibbs*, 1984, p. 39.

13. S. Piggott, 'Sir John Clerk and "The Country Seat"', in H. Colvin and J. Harris, eds., *The Country Seat: Studies in the History of the British Country House*, 1970, pp. 110–16. Clerk also visited Gibbs's 'fine Library' at Wimpole Hall, Cambridgeshire (note 10).

14. *Simpson*, p. 23, pl. 123.

15. *The Art of Architecture*, 1742, p. 15.

16. *Recueil des Plans, Profils et Elevations des plusieurs Palais, Chasteaux, Eglises Sepultres, Grotes et Hostels bâtis dans Paris* (the so-called *Petit Marot*), undated, with unnumbered plates.

17. Roger Gale to Maurice Johnson, 18 August 1739, in *The Family Memoirs of the Rev. William Stukeley, M.D.*, The Publications of the Surtees Society, 1882, III, p. 416.

18. *Simpson*, p. 22, pl. 70.

19. Adam dispensed with the central triangular pediment, which is a feature of Gibbs's published design though not of the drawing for it (Victoria and Albert Museum E.3602–1913), suggesting that he might have shown Adam some of the preparatory material for *A Book of Architecture* which was being made, with the assistance of his Scottish draughtsman John Borlach, in 1727.

20. T. Friedman, *James Gibbs*, 1984, pp. 133–35, 323, pl. 138.

21. Pl. 55. Campbell particularly noted (p. 3) the 'fine *Venetian* Window' of this elevation.

22. *Gifford*, pp. 128–31, *Macaulay*, pp. 89–90. Mar's design is illustrated in *Fleming*, pl. 8, where it is incorrectly given to William Adam.

23. Royal Institute of British Architects Drawings Collection J14/5/63.

24. Judged by Langley's own architectural compositions, such as the unsolicited entry for the London Mansion House competition of 1735, which he had some reason to believe would appeal to the City of London, as

Palladio was unwelcome there because he was neither a Protestant nor a Freeman (S. Perks, *The History of the Mansion House*, 1922, p. 171, plan 49). Compare this to Adam's Duff House, Banffshire, 1735 (*Simpson*, pp. 21–2, pl. 148).

25. *The Critical Review*, pp. iii–iv, viii.

26. p. 6.

27. 11 July 1734, p. 1.

28. *Piggott*, p. 116.

29. 18 July 1734, p. 1.

30. 14 November 1734, p. 1.

31. pp. 46–7.

32. 26 December 1735, p. 1.

33. *A Critical Review*, p. 42; *The Grub-street Journal*, 21 November 1734, p. 1.

34. 5 September 1734, p. 1.

35. *A Critical Review*, p. 11; *The Grub-street Journal*, 1 August 1734, p. 2: 'had this architect broke back his entablature over the capital of each column, unto the upright of the building (as is most scandalously done in the frontispiece to the *Meuse* [by Kent], the *Banquetting-house* at Whitehall, the gate of lord *Burlington's* in Piccadilly [by Campbell], and many other supposed fine buildings in London. . .I suppose, its mean aspect would have been in the elegant taste of our Critic [Ralph]'.

36. *A Critical Review*, p. 31; *The Grub-street Journal*, 3 October 1734, p. 2 and 18 July 1734, p. 1.

37. *Simpson*, p. 22, pl. 104.

38. 31 October 1734, p. 1 and 3 October 1734, p. 2.

39. 29 August 1734, p. 1.

All photographs by Leeds University Photographic Department.

What's His Line: Would the Real William Adam Please Stand up? Some recent research discoveries

Although William Adam's position as the 'Universal Architect'[1] of early Georgian Scotland is well established, his biographers' reluctance to address fully the significance of his business activities has led to an unbalanced portrait. New research, primarily focused on the Registers of Deeds at the Scottish Record Office, provides fresh evidence to adjust the parallax.

WHILE, from about 1720, William Adam consistently styled himself 'architect', to his contemporaries his acknowledged reputation was founded upon his wider talents; notably his entrepreneurial acumen. The eighteenth-century writers Sir John Clerk of Penicuik,[2] John Clerk of Eldin,[3] Sir Robert Douglas,[4] and the anonymous composer of Adam's obituary notice,[5] all emphasise his business interests. It is, therefore, somewhat surprising that given the relative accessibility of the materials for such a study, that modern authors like Fleming[6] in his pioneering account, and Gifford[7] in his recent biographical collage, have added little to our knowledge of this crucial aspect of Adam's career.

Not only was his own commercial success necessarily the financial foundation that carried Adam's architectural practice, if we are to believe his claim that he made a profit of only £300 on the building of Hopetoun House over the ten year period commencing 1736.[8] Indeed for some of his major patrons industrial activity and architecture were also closely correlated. In 1737 James, fifth Duke of Hamilton was keen to channel profits from his coal and salt works at Bo'ness (at which Adam was consultant troubleshooter) into building activity at Hamilton.[9] Some idea of Adam's business versatility may be gauged from the same patron's invitation in 1742 for him to visit Arran to assess and advise on possible industrial ventures there in spinning and bleaching, fisheries, and the exploitation of coal and mineral deposits:

> Since you know the succeeding in any project here that will bring in the pence, will make all edifices, obelisks, water works &c. &c. &c., go on the better at Hamilton. Therefore on the whole I think my advice for you to come hither is really what you should follow as it may probably prove so much to your owne advantage.[10]

But what of Adam's own ventures? The earliest and most comprehensive source of information regarding these pursuits comes from a travel journal kept by Sir John Clerk of Penicuik, who, upon visiting Kirkcaldy in 1728, conveniently listed them:

> I took a little time to consider a brickwork belonging to Mr Adams, Architect. This I found as expensive a piece of work as the nature of it

required and I could not enough admire the enterprising temper of the
proprieter who had at that time under his own care near to twenty
general projects—Barley Mills, Timber Mills, Coal Works, Salt Pans,
Marble Works, Highways, Farms, houses of his own a-building and houses
belonging to others not a few.[11]

Key documentation chronicling the progress of Adam's business and other interests is to
be found in the Registers of Deeds and their original warrants, housed at the Scottish
Record Office, and while space here allows no more than a cursory glance at a selection,
the material is given full consideration in my forthcoming doctoral thesis.[12] The relevant
local registers for Kirkcaldy[13] have proved a disappointing research tool in this instance
although Adam and his father-in-law, William Robertson of Gladney, do appear in minor
deeds. However, the general registers kept by the three Edinburgh offices,[14] unindexed
for the period 1700–1750, more than compensate, though to obtain the references it was
necessary to sift through some 750 000 entries in the minute books.

From many of the deeds, it is clear that Adam's elevation from mere mason in
Linktown was assisted particularly by his association with, at first, William Robertson
of Gladney. Later, Robertson's first four sons were each connected with Adam in the
expansion and diversification of his land and business transactions, by which time the
latter was clearly the dominant party. Robertson of Gladney had a string of industrial
enterprises, principally in coal and salt works, running right along the north shore of the
Forth from Culross to Methil.[15] From 1709 Robertson had a nineteen year lease on the
coal and salt pans of Kirkcaldy Links from Andrew Ramsay of Abbotshall and actually
resided at Abbotshall house itself before his removal to Gladney.[16] It was probably around
this time that Adam may have come into contact with him as one of the mutually
nominated wrights, smiths and masons appointed by Ramsay and Robertson to assess the
buildings on the estate.[17] At any rate, Robertson undertook to build colliers and salters
houses and salt plans in which Adam may have had employment (Fig. 1). It is clear that
Robertson was also familiar with the latest industrial technology,[18] and it was from him
no doubt that Adam gained the practical experience he was later to put to such
spectacular effect, notably at Pinkie[19] and Bo'ness.[20]

In a contract of employment engaging Mark Ovens 'worker in Tyle and Bricks', dated
at Leith 9 March 1716, Adam is designated 'Master of the Tyle Manufactory in the Links
of Kirkcaldy',[21] a venture he had entered into with Robertson of Gladney two years
earlier.[22] It is now possible to link them in another significant enterprise about this date
and clear up a long standing mystery.

Sir John Clerk of Penicuik's son, John Clerk of Eldin, in adding detail to the former's
list of Adam's business, gives specific credit to Adam for having brought a model of a
barley mill from Holland and thus introduced the making of pearl barley.[23] Since Clerk
of Eldin had first hand accounts of Adam's activities, his testimony is difficult to

1. Making Salt. The interior of this English pan-house is essentially the same as those managed by Robertson of Gladney and William Adam. From W. Brounrigg, *The Art of Common Salt* (1749).

discount.[24] Gifford's attempt to reconcile this, by conjecturing about Adam's possible involvement at the famous Saltoun barley mill[25] now seems less probable in the light of new evidence, though the identity of a 'Mr Adam' (not noted by Gifford) sent on a commission from a neighbouring laird to Henry Fletcher regarding the setting of a mill, remains open to further investigation.[26] Certainly by 1716 Adam was already 'Master of the Barley Manufactory of Edinburgh'[27] the location of which was stated by Robertson of Gladney as being 'at ye water of Leith'.[28] If Clerk's attestation that Adam's mill was indeed producing pearl barley is correct, then Shaw's claim that the Saltoun mill had a forty year monopoly can now be refuted.[29] The precise location of Adam's mill is difficult to pinpoint, but by using a combination of earlier surveys and Roy's map of c.1750, 'Bell's Mill' (just above the present Dean Bridge) seems to be the most likely candidate as qualifying for Edinburgh rather than Leith.

Adam's and Gladney's mercantile activities are illustrated in a charter party contracted at Alloa in February 1716 (Fig. 2), by which they engaged a ship to deliver salt from their own pans at Kirkcaldy and Wemyss to either Aberdeen or Portsoy and to return with a cargo of meal and barley to either Kirkcaldy, Leith or onwards to 'Caplagen' [?Copenhagen].[30] No doubt a voyage to Scandinavia would have meant a return cargo of timber and iron.

Some confusion has arisen from the surprising number of contemporary men of

2. Part of a *Charter Party* of 1716 by William Adam in which he designates himself 'Master of the Barley Manufactory of Edinburgh'. SRO RD 13/56/188.

3. Signatures from Deed Warrants at West Register House: (Top), William Adam, master of the card manufactory of Leith, 1714. (Middle), William Adam, saltgrieve at Cockenzie, 1716. (Bottom), William Adam, master of the tyle manufactory at Kirkcaldy Links, the future architect, 1716.

business sharing the name William Adam, appearing in the same location at the same time.[31] While several of them are easily discounted, two in particular have dogged research, but happily, original deed warrants are a failsafe means of avoiding embarrassing misattributions. The William Adam, salt grieve between 1716 and 1719 at the Cockenzie pans belonging to the estate of Winton[32] previously supposed to be the future architect, can now be discounted as a red herring, even though the error is understandable in view of the astonishing number of coincidences in their circumstances. Both shared interests in the salt industry, had associations with the Winton Estate through the York Building Company, links with Sir William Bennet of Grubbet, and other border connections around Kelso.[33]

The dates seem perfectly to explain Adam's activities prior to 1719 when he emerges onto the architectural scene as a supplier of bricks and iron to Alexander McGill at Donibristle.[34] The deed warrants disprove what hitherto seemed almost perverse to deny (Fig. 3).

Adam's industrial connections with the Robertson family continued, particularly with two of Gladney's younger sons, Archibald and Jerome. The two eldest, David of Brunton and James of Dowhill, were more involved in transactions involving Adam's ownership of various lands from 1723 till the 1740s.[35]

Jerome Robertson, designated 'merchant in Leven',[36] was an associate in Adam's timber and iron mills. In a lengthy contract of feu dated 1726, between them and

Alexander Gibson of Durie they purchased the lease of a 'Haugh of Land being part of [the] Barronys of Durie and Scoonie' close to some already existing corn mills by the Water of Leven.[37] Power was granted for the 'casting and running of Aqueducts to the miln already built by them upon the said Haugh of Land for the Slitting and sawing of timber'.[38] It is also apparent that they intended to build an iron mill nearby, possibly by converting the 'Bassmiln' in which case Adam was to provide a new corn mill as a replacement.[39] Adam's mills had priority for water power on certain days with a clause by Gibson to ensure that this could be overruled in order to guarantee the quotas of his own corn mills. Gibson also appeared to make a number of concessions to encourage this enterprise: all materials 'Livered or imported at his Harbour of Leven for the building of the said works and houses. . .shall be free of all shoar-dues', and in addition Adam was to take annual delivery of a quantity of coal from Gibson's works.[40] In return Gibson reserved the right to first refusal should any further partners be assumed in the venture. After the mill was established Adam paid annually a feu duty of fifty merks, £18 Scots, on all timber imported through Leven and one shilling Scots on each hundredweight of iron.[41] Adam was also bound by the agreement to manufacture sufficient plates for Gibson's salt pans, Gibson himself providing the materials. The sawmill was later the subject of arbitration when Adam and Robertson disputed their respective accounts, Robertson being ordered to pay Adam £8 214. 16s. 8d. Scots and to give in an inventory of all the timber at the mill.[42]

Adam also kept timber yards at Leith, a port more usually frequented by international shipping. A fair idea of his procedure in the importation of this commodity can be gained from the papers relating to his lawsuit from 1740–1745 with the representatives of one of his major suppliers, Charles Sherriff, merchant in Prestonpans, who died in 1740 leaving some business with Adam unconcluded.[43] Sherriff often dealt with Adam through Archibald Robertson who resided in his neighbourhood.[44] Incidental information from this source relates to Adam's marble works at Leith, then managed by Alexander Skirving.[45]

In 1722 William Robertson of Gladney was forced to give up his tack of the Abbotshall coal.[46] Sometime before the death of Robertson in December 1728, Adam had moved with his family to Edinburgh. 1728 is the pivotal year of Adam's career when great advancement was made in his official and personal status. Just one of the many changes occurring at this time was the switch in focus of his coal and salt interests to East Lothian. Adam's journey to London in the spring of 1727 has been presented in the context of his association with Sir John Clerk of Penicuik and his plans for publishing his designs. However, besides these considerations, Adam's stay in England extended well into August occasioned by his negotiations with the York Buildings Company[47] with whom he was to have a long association. By articles of agreement entered into between Colonel Samuel Horsey of Mortlake as Governor of 'the Company of Undertakers for raising

Thames Waters in York Buildings purchasers of the Estate of George late Earl of Winton' dated at London, 9 August 1727, the 'whole Colliery and Saltworks of Tranent and Cockenzie' were leased to Adam.[48] This lease gave him the ownership rights of all the colliers, coal-bearers, salters and their servants (who as serfs were transferable property),[49] all the gins, waggons, roads and utensils belonging to the works. Initially, Adam entered into a twelve year lease with an option to cancel with six months notice, at the end of each three year interval. In return Adam paid tack duty of 2000 tons of 'great coal', 3000 tons of 'mideling coal', or £250 Sterling per annum, payable at the London Office. The Company was also to have right of purchase of any coal sold from Adam's pits.[50]

In addition to coal and salt interests on the Winton Estate, Adam was in the process of setting up a related glass works at Portseton in 1728 and was also planning to erect an iron mill, in which case the York Building Company demanded an extra £50 rent.[51] This glasswork had the main objective of squeezing the Newcastle glass manufacturers out of business, according to Robert Dundas, who was one of Adam's partners along with the Earl of Stair and Lord Drumore.[52] This involved contracting for much of the kelp on the shores around Scotland, and particularly on the East Lothian coast, which was the main source of supply for the Newcastle companies, burned kelp providing potash, an important ingredient in making glass.[53]

Early in 1727 Adam became 'special errand bearer' and factor for the York Building Company on most of the Winton Estate,[54] an office he quickly deputised to his brother-in-law Archibald Robertson who seems already to have been manager of the coal and salt works of Tranent and Cockenzie.[55] Eventually Adam became full leaser of these two baronies including all the farms, tenants' houses in the town of Tranent, rights to the markets and fairs, town customs and duties, shore dues, anchorages of Portseton, its oyster beds and other fisheries, and granaries.[56] While granted power to extract stone, clay and sand (though not valuable metals), he also held half of 'Seton House' and its offices, owned by the company and was responsible for holding local courts and paying the minister's stipend.[57]

In 1742 Adam renewed his twenty-two year lease at Winton[58] and this was carried on by his son John after William's death in 1748.[59] This in no way diminished his interests in coal elsewhere. He was tacksman of the coal belonging to the Marquess of Tweeddale adjoining Newhailes, near Mussellburgh.[60] He advised widely on practical, engineering and economic improvements connected with the drainage of pits and increased productivity, notably at the Earl of Rothes's coal at Strathore in the 1730s (Figs. 4 and 5); the Countess of Eglinton's Ayrshire works, and the coal of Lochgelly belonging to the Elliots of Minto.[61] In addition he kept his own Fife works at Blair and Linktown working throughout the 1740s.[62]

The Registers of Deeds have also proved to be a particularly rich source of information

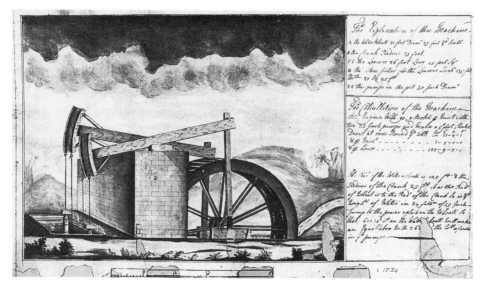

4. Colliery water engine at the Earl of Rothes's coal at Strathore c.1736. Though Adam advised on Strathore coal in 1736, this drawing is probably not by him, but is of the type of machinery familiar to him. Source: *Rothes Papers*.

other than Adam's purely industrial concerns. More personal material emerges too: as, for instance, the discovery amongst them of documents concerning Adam's claim before the Admiralty Court regarding a consignment of 104 reams of French paper from La Rochelle–such a quantity of high quality paper may conceivably have been intended for printing the plates for *Vitruvius Scoticus*.[63] There is also the exciting find of the original 'Decreet Arbitrall' made by Lord Tinwald which concluded Adam's protracted and painful lawsuit with Lord Braco.[64] John Adam's discharge to Braco for the contested sum, made only months after William's death, also survives.[65]

It is hoped that these important new items from the Registers of Deeds and related material given in this paper may show the way towards a more balanced assessment of William Adam's singular contribution to the spirit of the early Enlightenment.

University of St Andrews

ACKNOWLEDGEMENTS

I would like to thank His Grace the Duke of Hamilton for permission to quote from the Hamilton Papers at Lennoxlove; The Scottish Record Office for allowing reproductions from the warrants of the Registers of Deeds and from the Forfeited Estate Papers of Winton, in the University Library Muniments at St Andrews; Dr C.A. Whatley, University of St Andrews, Department of Social & Economic History for the illustration

5. A wind-powered version of a pumping engine at Strathore, c.1736. Source: *Rothes Papers*.

from Brownrigg's *The Art of Common Salt*; and Kirkcaldy Museum for the illustrations of machinery from the Rothes Papers in their care.

NOTES

1. Scottish Record Office, GD 18/4981, John Clerk of Eldin: 'Life of Robert Adam'.

2. SRO, GD 18/2108, Sir John Clerk of Penicuik: travel journal.

3. SRO, GD 18/4981, John Clerk of Eldin: 'Life of Robert Adam'.

4. Robert Douglas, *The Baronage of Scotland*. Edinburgh, 1798.

5. *The Caledonian Mercury*. No. 4325, 30 June 1748.

6. John Fleming, *Robert Adam and his Circle*. Edinburgh: John Donald, 1962.

7. John Gifford, *William Adam: A Life and Times of Scotland's Universal Architect*. Edinburgh: Mainstream, 1989.

8. Alistair Rowan, 'The Building of Hopetoun', *Architectural History*, 27, 1984, p. 194.

9. SRO, NRA(S) 2177/872, Duke of Hamilton to William Adam, 6 January 1737. The Bo'ness coal and salt was managed by Charles, 9th. Lord Elphinstone and George Dundas of Dundas: SRO, GD 75/530/1, 'Commission The Duke of Hamilton & Brandon to Charles Lord Elphinstone & George Dundas of that Ilk', 4 April, 1738. Adam's calculations on productivity and labour in relation to the use of horse gins, water gins and a 'fire engine' are detailed in SRO, GD 75/530/2, 'Note of Proposals for Additions and Alterations in working [the] Duke of Hamilton's main Coal at Bor=ness, to be considered upon by Lord Elphinston &c.', Dundas 14 February 1740. Adam's claim for expenses regarding this work is detailed in the claim made by John Adam against the Duke of Hamilton, SRO, GD 31/554 (Fea of Clestrain), 28 February, 1770.

10. NRA(S), 2177/872, Duke of Hamilton to William Adam, Castle of Arran, 29 June, 1742.

11. SRO, GD 18/4981, Sir John Clerk of Penicuik: travel journal.

12. William Adam (1689–1748): his Life and Work. University of St Andrews, Department of Art History.

13. SRO, B 42/7. Registers of Deeds, Kirkcaldy.

14. The relevant three offices are: Dalrymple, Durie, and Mackenzie. Minute Books, SRO, RD 7. Registers, SRO RD 2, 3 & 4 respectively. Original warrants are housed at West Register House, SRO RD 12, 13, & 14 respectively.

15. Robertson was tacksman of the coal of Valleyfield in 1702 as cited in David Beveridge, *Culross and Tulliallan*. Blackwood, 1885, p. 44. At the time of Adam's birth, Methil appears to have been the centre of Robertson's activities where he was a baron baillie: SRO, RD 2/70, 29 October, 1689.

16. SRO, RD 3/152. 'Tack, Ramsay & Robertson', registered 19 March 1718, dated 1709.

17. Ibid.

18. SRO, RD 4/1401/1. 'Discharge and Renunciation &c., William Robertson of Brunton In favours of the Representatives of Mr Andrew Ramsay &c.', 2 August 1726, Robertson (who had exchanged the lands of Gladney for those of Brunton, near Markinch, Fife, in 1723) mentions an inventory of 'all the engines, Salt panns, Salter houses and oyr materials I had built on the ground.'

19. Adam's 'bold stoke' at the Pinkie coal pits involved diverting water from the River Esk into a long tunnel excavated through solid rock at a depth of eight fathoms in order to obtain pressure to operate a water wheel. NLS, MS 14551 ff. 97–100, William Adam to the Marquess of Tweeddale, 14 September 1744.

20. SRO, GD 75/530/2, 'Note of Proposals'. NRA(S), 2177/2807;2810, monthly correspondence of Lord Elphinstone to the Duke of Hamilton concerning the Bo'ness coal, 1735–40.

21. SRO, RD 3/158, registered 11 June 1716; original warrant RD 13/56/188 dated 29 March, 1716.

22. Copy contract, 8 May 1714, Ramsay to Robertson and Adam, in Kirkcaldy Museum.

23. SRO, GD 18/4981.

24. Clerk of Eldin was William Adam's son-in-law.

25. Gifford, *William Adam*, p. 73.

26. Sir William Fraser, *History of the Carnegics Earls of Southesk*. Edinburgh: 1867, vol. 2, p. 285.

27. SRO, RD 3/148, 'Charter Partie, Adam & Crombie', Registered 25 May, 1716; original warrant RD 13/56/188, dated 22 February, 1716.

28. SRO, RD 2/166, 'Protest, Rig against Robertson & Adam', registered 14 May, 1722; dated 1 December, 1716.

29. John Shaw, *Water Power in Scotland*. Edinburgh: John Donald, 1984, p. 135.

30. SRO, RD 13/56/188, 'Charter Partie, Adam & Crombie', 22 February 1716, registered 25 May, 1716.

31. Some of these contemporary William Adams noted in the Register of Deeds include; the master of the school of Prestonpans (1709); a merchant in Culross, and his son of the same name (1712); the manager of the card manufactory at Leith (1714); the salt grieve at Cockenzie (1716); an apothecary surgeon of Edinburgh (1716); the schoolmaster at Linktown (1721); and a merchant in Kilsyth (1740s). All, at one time or another, have confused research!

32. C.A. Whatley, 'A Saltwork and the Community: The case of Winton, 1716–1719', *Transactions of the East Lothian Antiquarian and Field Studies Society*, 18, 1984, pp. 45–59.

33. Shortly after his removal from Cockenzie in 1719, William Adam salt grieve there was factor on the estate of Ayton (SRO, RD 4/128, 4 August 1720) and was empowered factor constitute for the York Building

Company on the estate of East Reston, Kelso by a deputation dated 29 November 1721: SRO, RD 2/117/2. William Adam, the architect, was engaged at this time on the remodelling of Floors Castle nearby. Both also shared associations with Sir William Bennet of Marlefield in Grubbet; the architect was nominated by him for the work at Floors. The salt grieve is mentioned in a letter to Bennet (who had links with the Commission of Salt and was an Officer of Customs and Excise) from Patrick Murray of Cherrytrees: SRO, GD 205/31/17, 8 December, 1717.

34. NRA(S), 0217 vol. 6, box 16, Earl of Moray MSS: 'Mr Alexr. McGill Dr to William Adam, for Bricks and iron &c.' 9 April, 1719.

35. SRO, RD 2/143, 'Disposition & Translation Robertson to Adam', 3 March 1738; Lands of Brunton, 1723. SRO C2/97/1 'Carta resig. Mr Guliemi Adams quaernend partinum Baroniae de Dowhill', 1740, Charter under the Great Seal.

36. SRO, RD 13/82/309, 'Contract of Feu 'twixt Alexr. Gibsone of Durie and Wm. Adam and Jerome Robertson.'

37. Ibid.

38. Ibid.

39. Ibid.

40. Ibid.

41. Ibid.

42. SRO, RD 13/73/273, 'Submission & Decreet Arbitrall Betwixt Jerome Robertsone and William Adam 1733.'

43. SRO, RH 15/38/63, Process: Sherriffs vs. Adam.

44. Ibid. 'Answers for Wm. Adam To the Petition of Sherriffs.'

45. Ibid. Letter, John Adam to Charles Sherriff, 26 April, 1740.

46. SRO, RD 4/140/1, 'Discharge & Renunciation Wm. Robertson to the Creditors of Abbotshall', 2 August, 1726.

47. For a history of the company see David Murray, *The York Building Company*. Glasgow: Maclehose, 1883.

48. SRO, RD 3/188, 'Contract 'twixt the York Buildings Company & Mr William Adam', registered 12 July, 1733; original warrant RD 13/73 dated at Beltonford, 2 December, 1729.

49. John Adam was later pursuer in a lawsuit over the ownership of fugitive colliers 'belonging to the Burgh of Dunfermline' along with, 'their wives and bairns' who had worked for William Adam at Pinkie. SRO, CS 237/A/1/72, Adam vs. William Murray, 1754.

50. SRO, RD 3/188, Contract, registered 12 July, 1733.

51. Ibid. Additional information about this glass manufactory is gleaned from William Adam's action before the High Court of the Admiralty concerning the arrestment and sale of utensils shipped from the works to Leith: SRO, AC 10/215, 'The Petition of William Adam, Architect in Edinburgh'.

52. SRO, GD 135/2217/4. Part letter, Robert Dalrymple to the Earl of Stair, n.d. [?1729].

53. Ibid. However, in 1741, all the glass for the additions by Adam to Carnousie House for Alexander Gordon was supplied by the 'Newcastle Company of Broad Glass'. SRO, RH 15/1/18, Account, 8 June, 1741.

54. SRO, RD 2/123, 'Factory, York Building Company to Adam', registered 25 January, 1728, dated 10 February, 1728.

55. SRO, RD 2/123, 'Deputation, Adam to Robertson', 10 February, 1728.

56. SRO, RD 2/123, 'Tack betwixt The York Buildings Company and Mr William Adams', registered 12 July 1733; original warrant RD 13/73, dated Edinburgh, 14 September 1728.

57. Ibid.

58. SRO, RD 2/158, 'Tack, York Buildings Company to Adam', registered 14 December, 1745, dated London and Edinburgh, 21 July & 5 August 1742.

59. SRO, RD 4/176/1, 'Copy Discharge, John Hamilton to John Adam', 2 February, 1750. Payment of tack duty for the Barony of Tranent for the year 1749–50.

60. SRO, RS 27/127, 'Renunciation, Marquess of Tweeddale & Wm. Adams To Sir James Dalrymple, Bart.', 15 November, 1742.

61. NRA(S), 744/40, Rothes Papers at Kirkcaldy Museum relating to Adam's role at Strathore. Adam's advice was sought about a waggon way at the Countess of Eglinton's coal in Ayrshire in 1735: Letter, Countess of Eglinton to Lord Milton, 29 November, 1735, cited in Sir William Fraser, *Memorials of the Montgomeries Earls of Eglinton*, Edinburgh: 1859, p. 360. The Lochgelly coal was surveyed by Adam in 1747: NLS, MS 13305, ff. 264–5, William Adam to Lord Minto, 18 July 1747.

62. SRO, GD 247/72/3 (John C. Brodie W.S. Coll.), papers relating to the coal at Blair, including letters to William Adam. Abbotshall coal was the issue of a 'Submission and Decreet Arbitrall twixt Adams & Arnott', 26 April 1745; SRO, RD 2/157.

63. SRO, RD 2/140, 'Submission & Decreet Arbitrall, Adams & Alexander', registered 28 November, 1736.

64. SRO, RD 13/88/334/1–3, 11 April, 1748. Papers from 1743–48.

65. SRO, RD 13/88/335, 'Discharge, John Adam to Lord Braco', registered 28 November 1748.

IAN GOW

William Adam: A Planner of Genius

Although English historians have tried to portray William Adam as an incompetent bungler this paper, through an examination and appreciation of his practical skills as a planner, suggests that a more sympathetic evaluation of his talents is long overdue and is intended as a warning to those who glibly apply English standards to the materially different world of early eighteenth-century Scotland.

THE simple elegance which has been so much admired in the architecture of early Georgian England was a consequence of the adoption of an elegantly simple plan of which Fig. 1 is an embryonic example. Compactness of outline, simple and pure geometric volumes held within a clear-cut matrix and harmonious proportional relationships between the parts are all characteristic of this approach. These are abstract concepts and no single aspect could typify this more than the emphasis on bilateral symmetry. It is customary to label this kind of plan 'Anglo-Palladian' but the cult of the beautiful plan is really an aspect of Neo-classicism.

If we turn to the survey of the state of architecture in Scotland which William Adam assembled as his *Vitruvius Scoticus*, while it is not true to say that we will search in vain for this kind of plan, exemplars among his own designs are few and far between. This led Sir John Summerson to dismiss the architecture of Scotland during the years after 1710 as being 'in a condition of remote provincialism from which it was not to emerge for half a century'. A kinder way of putting this would be to say that Scottish architecture differed from that of England. In this paper I intend to show that this difference was firmly rooted in Scottish plan forms.

Because William Adam was producing a different kind of building to that which was fashionable in England, it does not follow, as Fleming and Summerson regrettably imply, that he was an architectural bungler. Indeed I hope that this paper will convince you that Adam's skill in planning was the very mainspring of his genius. Before turning to Adam's own plans, however, it is worth pointing out that although early Georgian architecture has many admirers today, its preferred approach to planning was no guarantee of domestic comfort. A consequence of living in a geometrically generated grid is a degree of domestic sacrifice. If, for instance, you are standing in Room A, are you really any happier for knowing that Room B in the same position on the opposite side of the house has the identical disposition in mirror reverse? When Robert Kerr published his influential textbook on the planning of *The English Gentleman's House* in 1864, he began

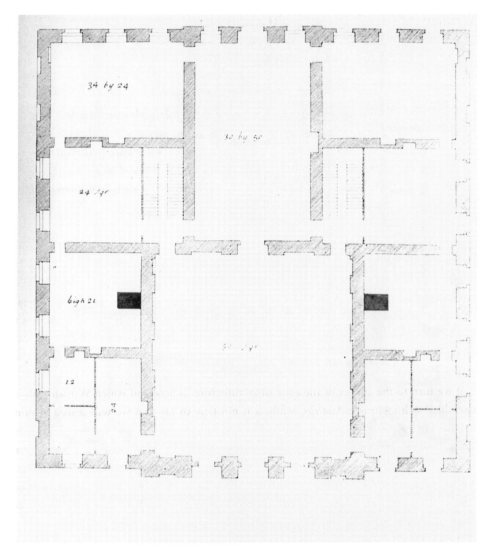

34 by 24

30 by 50

24 /y

high 21

50 /y

12

1. Design for a house dedicated to the Duke of Argyll by Colen Campbell from *Vitruvius Britannicus* 1715. Campbell's design is characteristic of the Anglo-Palladian plan with its great cube room and emphasis on bilateral symmetry in its paired staircases.

his analysis with a survey of the historical development of the plan of the English house and on reaching the Palladian phase confessed himself baffled. Although, as a trained architect, he was forced to concede that the Palladian plans produced an undeniable 'stateliness', he regarded the whole episode as an 'exotic' aberration by which he meant that it was something that flourished better in the warm climate of the Mediterranean.

Vitruvius Scoticus opens with the plans of Holyrood (Fig. 2). While the palace's primacy

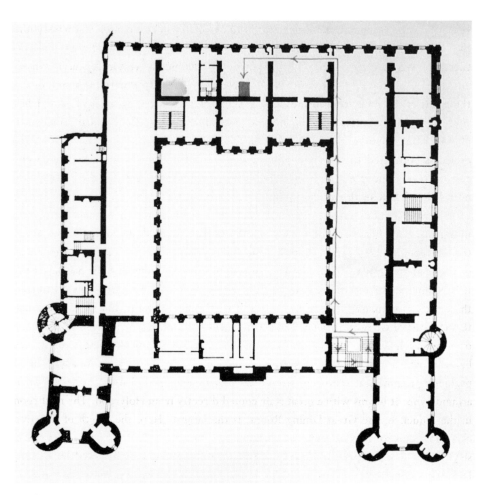

2. Plan of the principal floor of Holyrood Palace, Edinburgh designed by Sir William Bruce
c.1671. Modern survey by RCAHMS. The processional route through the Royal apartment
from the Great Staircase is indicated by the arrow and the position of the King's Bedchamber
in the centre of the garden front has also been marked.

in the history of Scotland's classical architecture is assured by the confidence with which
Bruce deployed the orders on its courtyard façades, the equal novelty of its plan has
perhaps been overlooked. The focus of the plan was the new Royal apartment on the first
floor approached by a grand staircase. Although some of the components of the great
chain of sumptuously decorated rooms are arranged in a practical way, in that it is
obviously convenient to have the King's close-stool room adjacent to his bedroom and
the Wardrobe next to the Dressing Room, the layout of the first rooms of the sequence
was primarily ritualistic. The following of Guard Chamber, Presence Chamber and so
on from the Great Stair, has its origins in Papal and medieval royal traditions, but at

Holyrood this arrangement had necessarily to be matter of self-conscious revival rather than survival because the palace had been grievously damaged in the civil wars. Holyrood therefore was a reassertion of royal power by the newly restored Stuart dynasty. Similarly, the King's cousin, Louis XIV, whose reign had begun with his humiliation at the hands of the mob, transformed the planning of Versailles into a board game whose rules were not dissimilar from the modern game of monopoly. The peculiar arrangement of these royal apartments was not solely for the benefit of the King, because in the degree of access permitted to different individuals it permitted dignity to be conferred on a sizeable body of people. The realities of Stuart government meant that the backstair was no less important in this arrangement.

This may seem to be straying from architectural problems but the success of Holyrood meant that a modification of the royal apartment was installed in country houses so that their owners could equip their more important guests with the necessary components of a ceremonial display. In Scotland a tradition of sound building in stone has meant that it is commoner to add rather than to build afresh, and it is thus often difficult to trace these state apartments in a confused mass of partly ancient walls, but we are fortunate that the Earl of Glasgow produced an arrangement at Kelburn which has all the economy of a lecture diagram (Fig. 3). Kelburn also demonstrates how the design of the new building was a result of the adoption of this predetermined plan. Arranged like a perfectly grammatical sentence, we see the components of a Scottish state apartment around 1700. It begins with a great stair copied directly from Holyrood. The next room in the sequence, the Great Dining Room, is the largest. Here the length of this great chain of rooms has been ingeniously curtailed by turning the Dining Room's rectangular shape through 90° where it breaks out beyond the façades. It is followed by a square Drawing Room and Bedchamber which connects to the backstairs. The backstair often permitted a servant's bedroom to be in close proximity by means of a mezzanine arrangement.

Incorporating this long run of rooms at the core of a Scottish house was a very considerable challenge to an architect's skills. The problem was that not only was the sequence of rooms rigidly fixed but even their sizes were more or less standard. An architect could occasionally introduce an Ante Room between the rooms which could conveniently take up some of the slack when old walls were involved but the only variable was the scale which reflected the patron's resources and ambitions. The dominance of the Great Dining Room must, I think, be directly related to the practical needs of current dining customs. Rooted in etiquette rather than aesthetics, it was the task of the architect to arrange his state apartment with elegance rather than to introduce novelties. Daring innovation exposed an owner to a degree of social risk and it is clear that the majority of patrons merely wanted to conform to the pattern. Architectural criticism, therefore, has all the thrill of watching competitive dressage or figure skating

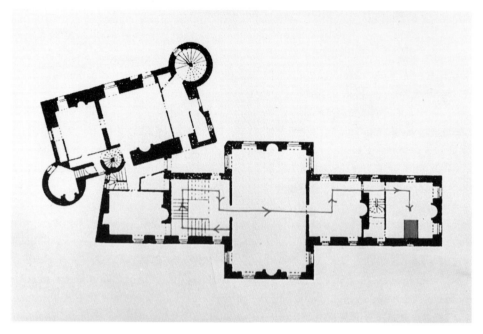

3. Plan of the principal floor of Kelburn Castle. Modern survey drawing by MacGibbon and Ross 1887–92. This shows the long new wing added to the old tower in the upper left hand corner by an unknown architect for the Earl of Glasgow around 1700 and shows how the plan followed from the predetermined sequence of rooms. Leading left to right from the Great Stair these are: The Great Dining Room, the Drawing Room, a Lobby, the State Bedroom with a Dressing Room off below the servant's stair leading to the valet's mezzanine bedroom.

and it is possible to award points accordingly. Without straying into the infelicities of its exterior resolution, Kelburn, I fear, would only scrape a C–because of the cramped nature of the Dressing Room. The best houses, like Holyrood, had an additional and yet more private Closet beyond the Dressing Room.

The architect of Kelburn is not known, but at Hopetoun we see Adam at the outset of his career. In *Vitruvius Scoticus* the plans logically precede the elevations and it can be seen easily that his primary consideration has been to impose a new state apartment on an existing house (Fig. 4). The scale of the Hopetoun apartment is stupendous and dwarfed that which Bruce had provided in the same area of the house. The plan cannot show the way in which its volumes break up above the floor levels of the rest of the house. The great size of the rooms may have been dictated by the need to display an important art collection because this was clearly a subsidiary function of the suite in most Scottish houses as Mackay's *Tour* describes. In my opinion, it is the block plan of the state apartment which has dictated Hopetoun's elevations. Although Adam produced a sequence which is functionally correct, even he could not contain its thrust within his

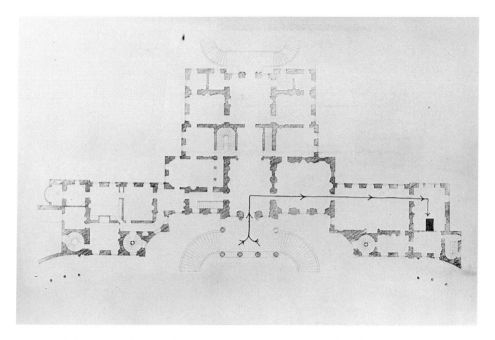

4. Plan of the Principal Floor of Hopetoun House by William Adam from his *Vitruvius Scoticus* around 1723. This shows that the State Apartment on the right has dictated the length of the new façade but, such is its extent, the State Bedroom has had to be contained in a single storey pavilion. Balancing it on the left are the luxuriously extensive private apartments of the Earl and Countess.

façades and the state bedroom had to be expressed as a single-storeyed pavilion, somewhat absurdly mirrored on the other side of the house where the slack is taken up by a balcony. For this reason Hopetoun, in spite of its size, can only be awarded a plain A.

If we turn from Adam's largest house to the smallest, Mavisbank, it is astonishing to find the same arrangement of rooms replicated on its principal floor (Fig. 5). Mavisbank is of outstanding importance because it was the house of a patron, Sir John Clerk, who was exceptionally literate architecturally, but it is important in this context because it was a new house on a virgin site and we can therefore see contemporary architectural aspirations untrammelled by the fashions of previous times. By arranging the state rooms in a circular fashion, Adam preserved the flow of the rooms without any functional distortion being imposed by the perimeter corset of the external walls. Because of this perfect grammar with both a dressing room *and* closet adjacent to the back circular stairs, I feel that Mavisbank in view of the degree of difficulty merits an A+.

Between the two extremes of Hopetoun and Mavisbank can be set the House of Dun which again is of particular interest because it too was a new building. In comparison

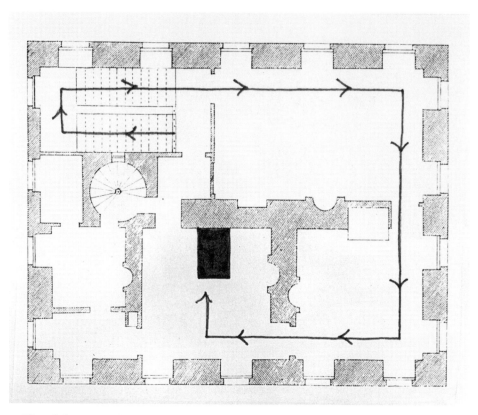

5. Plan of the Principal Floor of Mavisbank by William Adam from his *Vitruvious Scoticus* around 1723. This shows how ingeniously the standard sequence of state rooms was fitted into the confines of this tiny house by means of a circular clockwise arrangement.

to the Anglo-Palladian plan with which we began, at first sight, it appears to be a complete muddle, although the centrally placed 'Salon' suggests a stab at English fashions (Fig. 6). This room, however, is more usually referred to in the building papers as our familiar 'Great Dining Room', and the left-hand side of the plan is the state apartment, ingeniously shoe-horned into a compact and therefore economical plan. If we study the source of the superficially muddled look, it soon becomes clear that while each room in the sequence is well related to the next and is in itself disposed symmetrically, to squeeze so much in, Adam has had to juggle with the partitions and even shave walls away to win sufficient space for the main stair. An ingenious series of mural passages provides service access to each room in the suite.

Turning to the right-hand side we can see that this is given over to the family quarters and there has been no question of their comforts being sacrificed to the beauties of a publishable plan. Each room, however, possesses an integrity within itself which is most

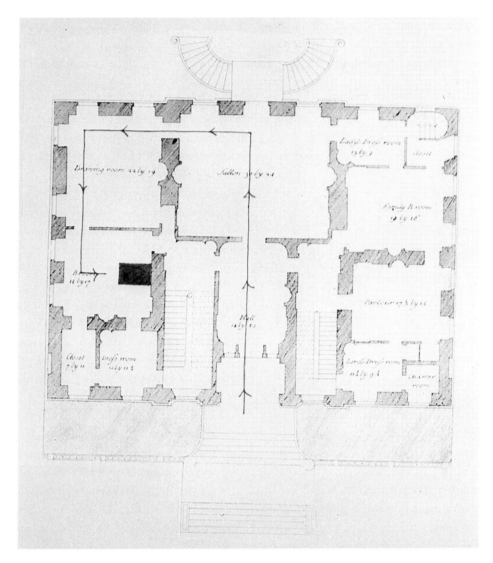

6. Plan of the Principal Floor of the House of Dun by William Adam from his *Vitruvius Scoticus* around 1728. This shows the State Apartment on the left balanced by the family's private rooms on the right. Although each room has its own internal symmetry, Adam has pared away walls and tunnelled through them with mural passages to ensure the necessary width for the main and convenient serive access.

obvious in the phalanx of three doors placed symmetrically across a single wall in both the bedroom and parlour. The plan cannot show the ingenious way by which the design operates in three dimensions. Dun has a complex variety of floor levels. The great Dining Room breaks up into the second floor with its deep cove and there are mezzanines on

69)

both staircases. A mural stair in the top right hand corner, reminiscent of tower house planning, connected Lady Dun's apartments to the nursery beneath them. As the *Vitruvius Scoticus* engraving shows, Adam's plan cannot be understood without a knowledge of the room functions. I think that once again we would have to award Dun an A+, although the Earl of Mar would merit a joint mention for his part in its formulation.

If we return to Hopetoun and focus on the left-hand side of the plan it is clear that this is an even more luxurious version of the private apartments noted at Dun. It is possible that the wives of many reigning German princes might have cast envious eyes towards the Countess of Hopetoun's suite with its large Dressing Room, which may have had plentiful wardrobe space, its closet and frescoed balcony. The key to Adam's success at a time when Scottish clients could easily have procured modish English designs must, I feel, lie in his skill in enabling Scotland's leading familiies to be both suitably grand and extremely confortable within the confines of their houses.

I hope that by this stage, you might feel that my title 'a planner of genius' has some justification and I could continue to portray plan forms to Adam's credit if we had time to examine either his many conversions of existing houses, or his small houses, like Minto in Edinburgh, both of which betray a fecundity of solutions to tricky planning problems. We can test his merits by measuring him against his architectural contemporaries because while Adam was undoubtedly the most successful, he was by no means the only architect practising in Scotland. These fellow designers remain shadowy figures but the recent discovery of the office drawings of John Douglas, allows a comparison. Although this design for additions to Archerfield (Fig. 7) shows a new type of house where the Dining Room and Drawing Room are given equal weight, it seems to me that Douglas lacks Adam's ability to weld the rooms into effective and economical relationships. One of Adam's greatest skills was his ability to give each room an internal symmetry of its own which was often the product of sleight of hand in the form of excavating into wall thicknesses or slimming down partitions when necessary. It is difficult to imagine Adam tolerating anything quite so awkward as this Parlour or Family Bed Chamber at Archerfield.

If we return to the point where we started, the divergence between Scottish and English plan forms cannot be simply the product of Adam's inferiority as Summerson would have us believe. Indeed, Robert Kerr, for one, might have taken Adam's part because his dismissal of Palladian planning cannot be applied to Scotland:

> The Basement Offices, the Great Hall and Saloon, the Portico, the symmetrical system of partitionment, the employment of detached wings, waste of space, undue pretentiousness at the expense of home comfort, still constitute the characteristics of the style; pedantic and fantastic forms of rooms are a common weakness; and one thing which is more singular than all else, as indicative of a positive want of skill, is the striking deficiency of ordinary Passages, and the readiness which is universally exhibited to

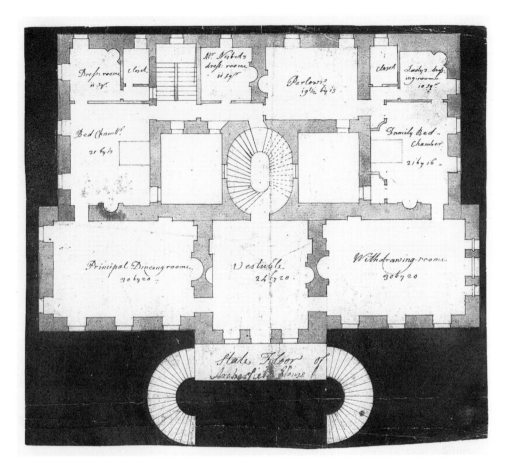

7. Preliminary design for the Principal or State Floor of Archerfield House by John Douglas, 1747. This plan shows how Douglas proposed adding a new wing to the front of the old tower house containing a symmetrical Drawing Room and Dining Room. Although it has been contrived with a measure of skill it seems very much less successful than Adam's plans and the rooms do not possess the same, apparently effortless internal symmetry.

create thoroughfare-rooms—not excepting even the chief apartments of the house.

Adam cannot be similarly faulted and seems to have struck an admirable balance between grandeur and family comfort on the principal floors of his houses.

Although Kerr was correct in assuming that the Palladian architecture of Lord Burlington had been directly informed by Italy through his possession of Palladio's drawings, I think that Kerr would have been surprised to know that at least one of his despised characteristics—the symmetrical system of partitionment—had its origins in a country as unexotic as Scotland. It can be seen in the architecture of James Smith who

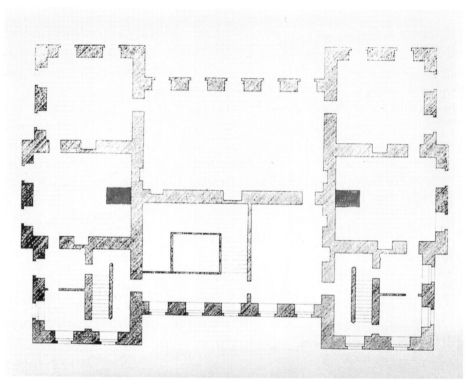

8. Plan of the Principal Floor of Melville House by James Smith 1697–1700 from Colen Campbell's *Vitruvius Britannicus* 1717. Although the Great Stair has been placed off the central axis, the plan shows a rigid bilateral symmetry in the paired apartments on either side of the central Saloon.

in some still little understood capacity acted as mentor to Colen Campbell. The plan which started this paper is 'English' only by publication because it was designed by Campbell, a Scottish architect, for a Scottish client, the Duke of Argyll. The same emphasis on symmetry can be seen in Smith's plan of Melville House (Fig. 8). Sir William Bruce may also have been interested in a symmetrical matrix, although the necessity of breaking it to fit in the state apartment means that it is less marked at Kinross than at Melville. The 'exact symmetry' of some Scottish houses was noted by Mackay, a professional country house visitor whose *Tour* was published in 1723 but, if *Vitruvius Scoticus* is representative of later Scottish taste, it is clear that it did not flourish and it was not an ideal that held much interest for Adam or his clients.

Indeed the attractions of this abstract ideal may even have been lost on Smith's clients because for all its symmetry of disposition, the upholsterer ensured that visitors to Melville were left in no doubt of the dominance of a single state bedroom as a visit to the Victoria and Albert Museum will prove. I cannot hope to resolve this fascinating conundrum. Among the factors which may be significant is that the greater wealth of England allowed for a more experimental, and often frivolous, architectural patronage whereas in Scotland the cost of building a house put such a strain on a family's resources that clients had to take a safe, long-term view of their investment. Adam's patrons, however, must represent a fruitful field for further research.

Summerson's accusation of provincialism does not apply if we widen our comparison and place Adam in a European, rather than the English, context. In France, architecture was subject to the same rationalist scrutiny that was applied to every aspect of scientific enquiry. Looking through French architectural publications it is clear that Adam is much closer in spirit to French ideas of comfort than Colen Campbell. The French upper classes seem to have enjoyed a much more sophisticated blend of that mixture of grandeur and comfort that we have seen at House of Dun. Adam, at Dun, had direct access to French ideas through the involuntary exile there of the Earl of Mar, during their collaboration on its design.

I want to end with a much more significant comparison:

> A proper arrangement and relief of apartments are branches of architecture in which the French have excelled all other nations: these have united magnificence with utility in the hotels of their nobility, and have rendered them objects of universal imitation.

These words are Robert Adam's and occur during his description of his plan for Syon House in his *Works in Architecture*, 1778. It is fascinating to reflect that the architect who rescued the plan of the English country house from its Palladian dead-end was William Adam's son. In dealing with an artist of Robert Adam's calibre it is pointless to speculate if his abilities were in any way inherited, and William's greatest gift to Robert was the cash which enabled the son to purchase the best architectural education that Europe could offer. I would argue, however, that the approach of both father and son is very similar. Both were interested in interiors and had a fondness for articulating them with architectural elements. Both attached great importance to the integrity of an individual room's symmetry. Their skills made them adept at converting old buildings and disguising their irregularities. Both had a taste for grandeur while at the same time their interest in conveniently relieving rooms by mural passages and jib doors made the magnificent comfortable. There was nothing provincial about the work of Robert Adam and it may be that his great advantage derived from having spent his formative years outside England, in Scotland and continental Europe.

The National Monuments Record of Scotland

The Practical Architect

The practical architect is not just a sound builder. Architecture which works should give pleasure, outside and in; it should provide accommodation which is well adapted to the purposes for which it has been produced; it should be strong, structurally sound and straightforward to maintain. A real architect contrives all three, not separately, but together, for Architecture which is worthy of the name is a synthesis of the Vitruvian precepts: Firmness, Commodity and Delight. William Adam was such an architect.

I HAVE to tell you straight away that I can't give you an unbiased view of William Adam. It's twenty years now since Alistair Rowan introduced me to him and since, rather reluctantly at first, I began the student dissertation which led ultimately to the 1980 reprint of *Vitruvius Scoticus*, with an introduction and notes to the plates. Colin McWilliam supervised the original study and I discovered the huge pleasure of working in the old National Monuments Record in Melville Street in what had been Sir Robert Lorimer's Dining Room, with Kitty Cruft sitting at her desk at the window answering all my questions. The best of academic godparents, they were, Alistair, Colin and Kitty; Modern Scottish architectural history owes them much, and William Adam and I could not have been luckier. Having been thus thrown together, William Adam and I, he became my eighteenth century hero and over the last twenty years my admiration for him has slowly but surely grown.

At least partly, I think, it has grown in parallel with my own experience as a practising architect, and it is from this particular viewpoint that I have been asked to approach the subject. I haven't really thought about this before, but I think it is a valid thing to do. There was a time when much architectural history was written by architects. Now that architectural history is an academic discipline in its own right, it is frequently written from a purely historical, or from an art-historical point of view. Who was William Adam? What did he do and how did he fit into the Scotland of his day? What were the sources of his architectural style and how did it develop as his career progressed? And what influence did he have on his contemporaries and successors, most notably, perhaps, on his sons? All of these issues are being considered by others or at least touched upon in one way and another in this volume.

My task is to try to look at William Adam not just as a 'good artist and a still better man', as the *Caledonian Mercury* obituarist described him, but as a real architect—as a producer not just of coloured drawings or black and white engravings on paper, but of buildings hewn and hoisted, levelled and laid, sarked and slated by masters and journey-men of every trade, not to mention seamen and sawyers, quarriers and carters, brick-makers and barrowmen. Real buildings made of dressed freestone and rubble, kiln burned and pit slaked lime mortar and harl; cargoes of trees and deals of 'Norroway fir' and wainscot oak, and of blue scleat or scailzie carried round the North coast from the Firth of Lorne; ingots of lead dragged along the new carriage road from Lord Hopetoun's mines at Leadhills and cast into sheets on sand bedded casting tables set up in basements; lime and gypsum stucco modelled *in situ*; tin glazed tiles shipped from Delft; cylinder and crown glass from London and Newcastle, and the occasional special order of polished bevelled Vauxhall plate; blacksmith made nails and cramps, straps and hinges; locks, bolts, knobs and handles from the brassfounder and locksmith; best Italian and Belgian black marbles; hand ground pigments, bound in oil and laid on a white lead ground. For these were indeed real buildings, skilfully brewed and cask conditioned; nothing like the factory produced gassy keg variety of later years!

William Adam was no mere drawing board architect. As we have seen, he did not only design these buildings; he was the undertaker, that is he undertook or contracted for the construction of many of them. He had trained as a mason, the dominant building trade; he had established his own brick and tile works in 1714 and he traded as a merchant in nearly all the materials and components of which great buildings were made. His knowledge and understanding of the building business was therefore total, and indeed to a great extent he appears to have dominated, perhaps even controlled, the Scottish construction industry, and like builders in all ages, he made a lot of money.

But to deserve to be called a 'real architect' one does not, I think, require to be a builder. William Adam's trade and mercantile career, though it continued to parallel and complement his architectural career throughout his life, was merely the foundation on which the latter was built. History is, after all, full of commercially successful merchants and tradesmen, very few of whom have professional, cultural, intellectual or artistic aspirations, except possibly as patrons. William Adam was different; he was a small man, fit and energetic, attractive, articulate and sociable. I often wish he could join some of us for an evening in Bannerman's at the foot of Niddry's Wynd, on, or at least close to, the site of his coalyard, across the Cowgate from Adam's square; I think he would be good company, and would enjoy the professional gossip—much of it about himself in recent months—in that rather architectural alehouse. He was also devastatingly bright, not in a scholarly but in a creatively practical sort of way. He must once, I think, have been the sort of little boy who always wanted to know how things worked and who made models.

He was clearly fascinated by what he saw as a young man in Holland and Flanders; the canal between Ostend and Bruges and the raising and lowering of seagoing ships in the locks; the houses with shaped gables, built of brick and with pantiled roofs; a new type of barley mill for making pearl barley, way beyond anything he had seen at home. He probably also saw Amsterdam town hall, built of Scots stone, the Mauritzhuis and perhaps Het Loo, great gardens with purely ornamental canals and water works: all much more sophisticated than anything he had seen in impoverished Scotland, still reeling from the near famine years of the 1690s, the effects of the Navigation Acts and the Darien failure, the arguments and machinations which culminated in the Union. But a young man who had been baptised in the name of William in 1689 was unlikely to have had Jacobite tendencies and was likely to take a favourable view of the Union and the securing of the Hanoverian succession. His sympathies, attitudes, interests and enthusiasms were right for the time: the opportunities were there, and he took them.

William Adam's optimism, his enthusiasm for technological innovation and the influence of his time in the Netherlands show themselves at the beginning of his independent career: the Saltoun barley mill* and Gladney House, both of 1711, when he was twenty two, and the Linktown brick and tile works three years later. If Gladney was roofed with imported pantiles from the start, which is at least a possibility, it would have had, with its shaped gables, a consciously Dutch aspect, though the details were derived from the work of James Smith. If I am right in postulating a date of about 1715 for Makerstoun, Roxburghshire, then it is William Adam's earliest country house design and the only one to pre-date the 1715 first volume of *Vitruvius Britannicus*; it is firmly in the manner of Smith, but with an idiosyncratic shaped pediment (Fig. 1). In these early designs, William Adam seems to me to be still very much the amateur, the promising young mason from Linktown, already acquiring a reputation as a capable builder, but without, as yet, much knowledge or understanding of the intellectual side of architecture. He could not yet claim to be a real architect. It seems to me that it must have been *Vitruvius Britannicus* which changed all that.

Campbell's *Vitruvius* was very much a manifesto, designed to promote neo-Palladianism as the style for Whig, Hanoverian Great Britain. It was bound to appeal to an ambitious young Scot who saw the opportunities which the Union—a bit like 1992—offered; not least a new group of patrons who would wish to demonstrate their influence and power through houses and villas in the new manner. To romantic 1990ish Scots with nationalistic tendencies, this may seem unattractive; but one only has to read certain passages in Baron Clerk's 'The Country Seat' to appreciate that there was at least as much idealism on the Unionist as on the anti-Unionist side in early Georgian Scotland: Great Britain was a noble concept, heralding peace, prosperity and enlightenment in a new Augustan age—which in a sense it was. William Adam's architecture was to give expression to the ethos of early Georgian North Britain. To put it less pompously, an

---

* William Kay has pointed out that William Adam built a mill on the Water of Leith and that he may not—as John Gifford has suggested—have been connected with the Saltoun Mill.

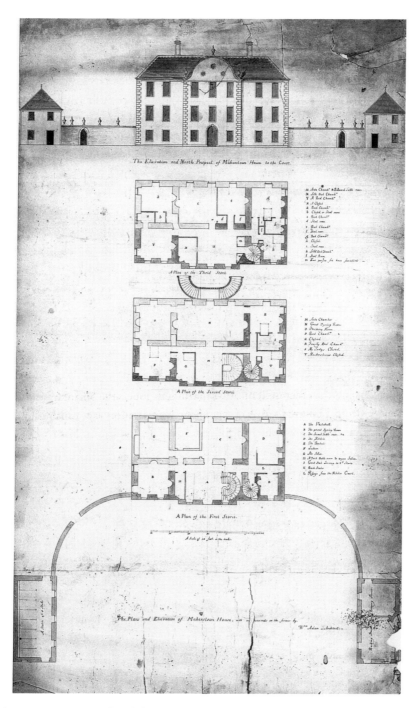

1. Makerstoun House, Roxburghshire, Plan and Elevation by William Adam, probably circa 1715. (Permission to reproduce this drawing is gratefully acknowledged to Christopher Scott Esq., of Gala.)

architect wants to be able to build, and needs patronage to do so; it is in that sense and by that mechanism that architects respond, and architecture stands for and represents, not just the architects, but the society which produces it.

To be judged fully, architecture must be judged according to the ancient precepts of Vitruvius: Firmness, Commodity and Delight. Architecture which works should give pleasure, outside and in; it should provide accommodation which is well adapted to the purposes for which it has been produced; and it should be strong and structurally sound, sensibly and well contrived and straightforward to maintain. A real architect contrives all three, not separately, but together, for Architecture which is worthy of the name is a synthesis of the Vitruvian attributes.

The practical architect is not just a sound builder; an ugly building tends to become progressively unloved, uncared for, unwanted and unsound. That William Adam's buildings give pleasure to all sorts of people at all sorts of levels and in all sorts of ways, is undeniable. 'The Pillars' in Dundee was the heart of the town (Fig. 2); there the old men would gather to shelter from the rain, smoke their pipes and blether; you can't do that in City Square, the bleak urban space which replaced it, despite the recent so-called environmental improvements. But its powerful image, so expressive of early Georgian civic pride, which once closed the view down Reform Street, now serves in model form as the hanging sign for at least two pubs. Only the notoriously poor quality of Dundee stone was its undoing.

The country houses offer delight in numerous ways: the scale and totality of the concept, so extensively described in Baron Clerk's poem 'The Country Seat', to which William Adam's houses give physical expression. The sheer quality of the landscape designs, semi-formal schemes, brilliantly adapted to the topography. The gardens at Newliston and at Hopetoun have survived remarkably, though much needs to be done; walking through Hopetoun's wilderness garden, the alignment through the North East bastion onto Blackness Castle and the subsequent panoramic views of the Firth of Forth are, literally, revelations and sheer delight. Revealing in a different way, is the fact that his sons instructed Hopetoun and Chatelherault to be conjoined in the relief panel carved, probably by Henry Cheere, for his Greyfriars tomb. As things turned out at Hamilton Palace, perhaps it's a pity that Chatelherault isn't over towards Abercorn but, that apart, is there a more skilfully contrived and spectacular viewstopper anywhere in Britain?

A glance through the pages of *Vitruvius Scoticus* may give the impression that the houses are rather alike; in fact it is the style of the engraving rather than the architecture which creates this illusion, and Dalmahoy, Haddo and the Drum, while perceptibly from the same stable, are quite different in aspect; the architectural language may not change, but the dialect, the pace and the volume certainly do. Each house has its own mood, its own personality. William Adam's elevations may be thought by some art historians to lack

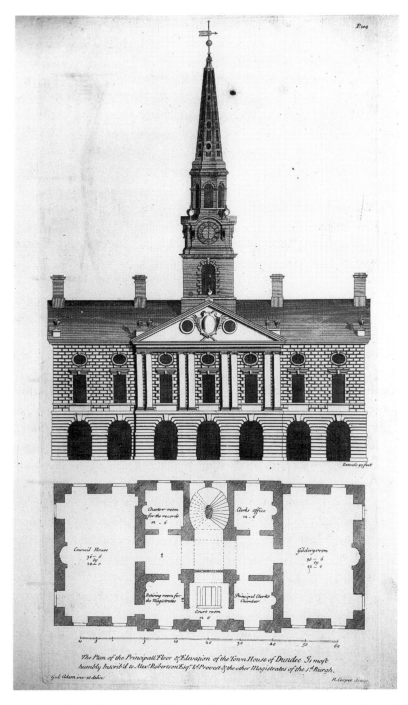

2. Dundee Town House designed by William Adam in 1731, built 1732–5, and demolished in 1932.

reason and consistency, and to defy categorisation as either Palladian or Baroque. By others they are seen to have a refreshing unpredictability; to be bold and vigorous; neither clumsy nor crude; British yet recognisably Scots; serious, yet never dull.

William Adam's interiors generally also work well aesthetically. He understood space and light. Though his plans are generally deep and double pile, tripartite or a combination of two, his use of double volumes and of stairs, tribunes and upper halls, which are top lit from roof lanterns or cupolae, gives a rich spatial quality to most of his interiors. Added to this can be that other sort of richness which is provided by joiners and carvers, plasterers and painters. Both types of richness are present in full measure at Arniston, where the double volume hall, the top lit main and service stairs and the boldness of Joseph Enzer's plasterwork exemplify the sort of atmosphere and effect which William Adam must have liked to create. His rooms are as individual as the outsides of his houses, where again one might think at first that they were variations on a single theme. Some have pine panelling, plain painted or decorated with trompe l'oeil or grisaille landscapes by James Norie, others have rich plasterwork on walls and ceilings. It was a matter of general principle that doors, windows and fireplaces had to be symmetrically disposed and that the chimney, lined with Delftware tiles and often with an integral overmantle, all in marble and supplied ready to build from his own warehouse and yard in Leith, was always the central focus of the room. Further research may show that William Adam was one of the first to use mahogany for doors and stair bannisters and handrails—for example at the Drum and Mavisbank in the late 1720s.

So much for delight, but what of commodity? It is not given to all architects to be good planners—I mean planners of the circulation and rooms within buildings. Planning is a bit like chess: you move one piece or one room, or change one function and the whole game changes. The planning of early Georgian houses was subject to certain conventions: stable and kitchen offices, service rooms and servants' accommodation, family rooms, library and billiard table rooms all had to be provided in suitable relationships one with another. Pride of place was given to the State Apartment, that sequence, following or suite—depending on whether you prefer Latin, English or French—of Great Dining Room, Withdrawing Room, State Bedchamber, Dressing Room and Closet, which was successor to the medieval Hall and Chamber and which survives vestigially in many of our own houses as the spare bedroom. If the State Apartment was above the entrance or vestibule floor, as it often was, even in such small houses as Mavisbank and the Drum, there was a State Stair, a formal ascent from the entrance Vestibule to the lower end, as it were, of the Great Dining Room. This left a need for a second or service stair connecting all the floors, ground to attic, from which servants could appear, as if from nowhere, in any room. To achieve this, while at the same time keeping the windows regularly placed, both in the rooms and on the elevations, and the fireplaces and flues in the internal spine and cross walls, was like solving a three-dimensional Chinese puzzle. William Adam revelled in this sort of planning, and where he shows himself as a real architect, not just as a drawing board architect, a two-dimensional pattern maker or a graphics man, is in his apparent ability to conceive and carry the three-dimensional design of a house in his mind; I say this because I believe his houses work functionally and visually even better in reality than they do on paper; what sometimes look like awkwardnesses on the plans are nothing of the sort. Sometimes architects fool their clients, and even deceive themselves with their own drawings: as Clerk wrote in 'The Country Seat': 'For oft tis known that a well finished draught deceives the eye, and ushers in a train of disproportioned labours and of endless pain!' Though he was a perfectly capable draughtsman, to William Adam it was the building and the rooms that mattered, and the land form, the natural features and the prospects and the controlling of them by siting and planting, never the designs on paper as mere abstract patterns for their own sake. He was, as I say, a real architect.

And so we return to the first of the Vitruvian attributes: Firmness. However delightful, fashionable and photogenic a work of architecture may be and however well it provides for the functions which it is required to accommodate, however comfortable and well equipped it is, if it is not structurally and constructionally sound, the whole thing is a complete waste of time. Firmness is the first and fundamental requirement.

As I said at the beginning, William Adam knew about building; about land surveying and civil engineering, about the design of roads, canals and bridges: The Tay Bridge at Aberfeldy was simply the most architectural of many; his great eighty-foot semicircular arch at Cullen is a simple masterpiece. He knew about soil mechanics and foundations and all that there was to know about masonwork. He almost certainly knew of the work of Christopher Wren and Robert Hooke on the design of roof trusses and composite floors for covering large spans. Whatever his precise role in it, the Saloon floor at Yester, the principal beams of which span thirty feet with the aid of iron tension rods, was up to the minute technology. The use of lead in combination with West Highland slates had, by William Adam's time, greatly extended the possibilities of roof coverings. This in turn made double pile, tripartite and more complex deep plan configurations feasible as they had never been before. Hopetoun could never have been roofed without extensive use of lead, so it was a convenience, to say the least, that Lord Hopetoun owned the lead mines. It was lead, too, that made possible the covering by an upper platform of what had previously been an 'M' or hopper roof on Yester. The plumber who cast and laid this roof was John Scott, and we know from the Duff House lawsuit papers that he also laid the original lead roofs on Arniston. This was particularly attractive information to me, for I and my firm were responsible for overseeing the re-laying of both these roofs about ten years ago.

Actually working on William Adam's buildings, and I have since worked at Hopetoun and at Tinwald in Dumfrieshire, has, I must say, concentrated my mind and has enabled me to look and to see things I would never otherwise have appreciated. It has also given me a very considerable respect for William Adam and his craftsmen, so many of whom are identifiable from manuscript letters and accounts and from the Duff lawsuit papers. We know from the latter, to quote one example, that John Meldrum, journeyman mason in Edinburgh, was employed by William Adam between 1727 and 1743 at Airdrie, Duff, Cumbernauld and Drum, at all of which houses John Burt was foreman mason, and at Hopetoun under Walter Mories; at the time of his evidence in 1743, he was working for William Adam on Edinburgh Castle. This feeling of proximity, of intimacy, almost, with the buildings and the men who made them is, quite simply, a good experience.

The construction of William Adam's houses is, in principle, simple. The house is likely to be in three parts, a centre block and two pavilions, one containing stables, the other kitchen offices: but there are many variations on this theme. Below ground, there will be a fairly elaborate system of stone built drains and conduits or cundies, including, usually, a perimeter drain into which the lead rainwater conductors discharge. The walls may be generally of stone; where this was rubble it was designed to be plastered or harled. The basement or ground storey, which depended on a great deal of ventilation to keep it dry, was normally vaulted and plastered internally directly onto the masonry. The vaults, sometimes the internal walls, and at Tinwald all but the outer facing stones may be of brick. The flues will normally be all in internal walls, which, with a number of fires burning will have become effective heat reservoirs.

The upper floors and minor partitions will be of timber and all the rooms on the entrance floor and above will be lined with lath and plaster or panelling. The vestibule floor may be of stone or marble, laid on the vault. Internal joinery will normally be of painted Baltic pine, except for the grandest doors and stairs, which may be mahogany. External joinery, doors and window sashes are likely to be oak. Roofs will be of slate and lead on boards over sometimes quite elaborate assembly marked roof structures. Cast iron gutters and pipes had not been invented, so rainwater is normally collected in lead lined cornice gutters, or behind parapets or balustrades and discharged into lead hoppers and conductors and thence to the drains. It is all very simple and rational, post-medieval, but pre-industrial. It was a coherent system of construction and, in a house which was fully staffed and managed, it offered a high degree of comfort; it was also maintainable. Where these houses have got into trouble, it has usually been through neglect of the roofs and rainwater systems, often in the hard middle years of the present century. One must hope that such neglect is at an end. The fundamental firmness of William Adam's houses, and of his other buildings is never, in my view, in doubt.

So how does all this leave this architect's assessment of William Adam, as a practical architect? I am, as I said at the outset, much too involved with him to be objective, but if firmness, commodity and delight are the right criteria, I find it hard to mark him down on any count. He was clearly widely liked and respected in his day. His neglect since then is surely a matter of fashion; of a sort of assumption that his London contemporaries are bound to have been more important; of a certain snobbishness which misrepresented him as a tradesman; of a romantic tendency to reject Unionists and Hanoverians; of a failure to recognise him as a significant figure in the context of the Enlightenment. I don't know; all I can tell you is that for all the reasons which I have tried to give you, I think very highly of him indeed. He was a highly practical architect, he was, moreover, a real Architect.

Simpson & Brown, Architects

ALTHEA DUNDAS-BEKKER

The Patron's Part—Living in a William Adam House 1726–1989

William Adam's Patron, Robert Dundas is introduced and the heirs who follow him and their alterations to the house to suit their own individual needs.

ROBERT Dundas (Fig. 1) commissioned William Adam to draw up plans for a new Mansion House at Arniston in 1726. Patron and architect were around the same age, both men in their forties. Dundas's contemporary, Dr Carlyle of Inveresk, writes this description of the patron: 'His appearance was against him, for he was ill looking, with a large nose and small ferret eyes, round shoulders, a harsh croaking voice, and altogether unprepossessing,' however, Carlyle continues, 'by the time Dundas had uttered three sentences, he raised attention, and went on with a torrent of good sense and clear reasoning, that made one totally forget the first impression'. Nor were his habits conducive to hard work or attention to business. According to another contemporary writer, 'he was naturally averse to study and application and (except when employed in the practice of his profession) consumed his time in convivial meetings, and the company of his friends and acquaintance'. When he commissioned Arniston, he was rising very rapidly in his legal career. In 1717 he had been appointed Solicitor General, and in 1720, Lord Advocate. But he was dismissed from office in 1725 after falling out with Sir Robert Walpole over the Malt Tax, so he returned to Scotland where there was now time to turn his attentions to the building of a new family mansion house. At the end of his legal career he held the post of President of the Court of Session, as indeed did his son later on; the Dundases therefore wielded great power in Scotland in the eighteenth century. When his son went off to Utrecht University, Robert Dundas cautioned him not to enter too much into the taste of throwing money away on books; 'when that turns a disease, 'tis as bad as pictures'. Conversely, Sir John Clerk of Penicuik had admitted in his Memoirs that he 'understood pictures better than became his purse'. It has been suggested that at Mavisbank the knowledgeable Sir John Clerk placed considerable constraint on the Adam plans, but at Arniston, the Dundases being pretty clueless culturally, Adam had complete licence, especially in the hall, to do as he liked. He also did plans for the gardens looking to the south, including an elaborate parterre and a cascade, the waters of which would build up in a pond half way up Castleton Hill and could be let off for a period of half an hour, tumbling over white stones, whilst being watched by Robert and his friends dining in the Oak Room. All this was completed by 1732, but unfortunately was the cause of funds drying up, leaving unfinished a third of

1. Robert (first President Dundas of the Court of Session) who commissioned William Adam to draw up plans.

the main block which had been scheduled for the laird's sleeping apartments on the ground floor, a couple of staterooms on the first floor and also the external walls. This odd toothless gap effect was to remain for 20 or so years.

In 1748 Robert died and his eldest son, Robert, inherited. The new heir was at once to depart from the William Adam plans, as did every following generation–it is human need to assert identity in one's place of abode. I can quite understand that, given the enormity of merely inheriting, probably not even deserving, something as monumentally lovely as a William Adam house, one could be thought a little greedy to be, in addition to owning Arniston, feeling the need to make alterations to it. What a very large slice of life's cake! But if this is the case, I have to say that each and every Dundas generation therefore, since 1726, has been having a jolly big munch. The waters of the South Esk have flowed past many generations of the family at Adam's Arniston, and they all appear to have felt this same human need, as each one has executed some sort of a change at Arniston in accordance with different attitudes to living. Now, I am simply going to describe the changes and the personalities involved, without justifying, though I often do at Arniston, usually when remarks have been passed on the unsuitability of the present

2. Robert (second President Dundas of the Court of Session) from a painting by Raeburn.

north porch, or criticising either, which I frequently do when remarking on the unsuitability of the north porch of the house!

Robert is our next personality; he attended Utrecht and like his father became President of the Court of Session (Fig. 2). The Dundas men appeared also to have inherited the good fortune of marrying very pretty and, much more importantly, supportive wives:

> Henrietta, gracious, affable, Modest, justly kind,
> Whose face displays the Beauties of her noble Mind,
> Indulgent, smiling now in a comely wedding dress,
> May heaven her Life with every Bounty still Bless.

The author asks 'Let me know if this may be printed and published', but it appears the hint was not taken as it exists only in the original manuscript. Henrietta Baillie was heiress of Lammington and Bonnington estates and very rich. Robert writes in his diary miserably at his succession:

> I found affairs much encumbered with a great load of debt provision to seven younger children, most of them young and still uneducated. I was relieved by a few words from one of the most sensible, amiable, and affectionate women that ever made a man happy, who spoke these words:

86)

3. Arniston House from the southwest.

'Take up your succession without hesitation, keep your father's estate, be kind to and educate your younger brothers and sisters, finish the house and policy about Arniston, it looks ill in its present situation; surely my estate and yours together will leave an opulent succession to our children; if necessary sell a part of mine, I will execute any deed you require'.

The toothless gap on the west of the main block was awaiting William Adam's two staterooms, and the Laird's sleeping apartments. The two new generations, the Dundases, and the Adams in the form of John, abandoned that idea. The staterooms had originally and rather impetuously, been planned in excited anticipation of a royal visit, but by the 1750s it was realised that the royal family showed little inclination to visit Scotland, let alone Arniston. John Adam used the area for a drawing room and dining room at ground floor level, with bedrooms up above. Unfortunately, this area is now gutted due to an outbreak of dry rot in the 1950s. Eighteen years of restoring other areas of the house have stretched resources so the John Adam drawing-room and dining-room still wait a re-instatement.

The next heir is the eldest son of the second marriage, to Jean Grant of Prestongrange, little, alert, handsome, gentleman-like, with a countenance and air beaming with sprightliness and jollity, and dignified by considerable fire; altogether inexpressingly pleasing Robert, whom we differentiate from the others by calling the Chief Baron, because he was, of the Exchequer. That was Lord Cockburn's description of him. But

4. Arniston: the two pillars topped with perching cougars.

there was a complaint about his stature in Parliament from Mr Ferguson of Pitfour, who was member for Aberdeenshire, when Dundas came to be Lord Advocate. Ferguson complains, 'the Lord Advocate should always be a tall man. We Scotch members always vote with him, and we need therefore, to be able to see him. I can see Pitt and Addington, but I can't see this Lord Advocate'. Robert married his cousin, Elizabeth, eldest daughter of Henry, Viscount Melville. He executed very interesting changes to Arniston. When old Parliament House was being rebuilt at the end of the century, the stones from the old frontage were being treated as mere rubbish. Robert rescued them and brought cartloads out to Arniston and there they were incorporated into ornamental doorways and bridges about the pleasure grounds. Most interesting was the Royal Arms which was built into the new south pediment (Fig. 3) behind which Robert installed a schoolroom for his children, right at the very top of the house. On the present B6372, at the end of the Arniston Beech Avenue, stand two old pillars topped with perching cougars (Fig. 4). When Robert was a small boy at the High School he used to pass them in Nicholson Street. Later, when that house was being pulled down and they were up for sale, Robert bought his old friends and had them installed at Arniston.

His heir Robert, born in 1797, was to leave the profession of law with which the family had been connected since 1600 (Fig. 5). However, he redeems himself by having the distinction of being the only really good-looking member of the Dundas family, and

5. Robert Dundas, born in 1797, who was to leave the profession of law.

he also married an heiress. Lilias Calderwood Durham who owned the estates of Polton near Lasswade, and Largo in Fife. It may be that he did not actually do any changes at Arniston, whatsoever, although we are rather vague as to when the porch on the south side of the house was added (Fig. 3)–it could have been by the time of his death in 1838 when he was only forty-two. It was within his lifetime that the lime avenue was planted on the drive which we now all use, which brings the visitor up to Arniston and the north porch. His heir, Robert, my great-grandfather, explained this addition in his diary. He said he was sorry to do it but a Scottish country house in winter needed a porch. He also, in 1877, added a second storey to the colonnades which join the wings to the main body of the house. In this way, access was gained to the bedrooms in the East Wing, and the new corridor was fitted up with bookcases as an extension of the library shelves. At the time of the building of the North Front Porch, Mr Wardrop, the architect, observed the weatherworn state of the family arms in the pediment at the top of the house. It was found to be badly crumbling to the extent of being a danger to people walking below. The entire building as low down as the capitals of the pillars was taken down and rebuilt.

89)

None of the old stones were used again, stone from Doddington Hill near Wooler being used instead, which closely resembled in colour that of which the house is built.

In summing up, I return to the title 'The Patron's Part–Living in a William Adam House 1726–1989'. I hope in the short space allowed I have dealt fairly adequately with the 'Living' bit, not quite up to 1989 I know, but that is going to get a mention. 'The Patron's Part' I have probably dealt with less successfully–having the gall to describe what at best might be called carrying out slight departures from William Adam's plans, and at worst, Dundases doing unspeakable things to listed A buildings. Some of it though is surely praiseworthy. Our own adaptions have been to consolidate our day-to-day living to just one storey, the first floor, which involves, if we want privacy, simply shutting William Adam's doors. We also created a kitchen out of what was rather a horrid little closet, which I am sure had nothing to do with Adam. I can report no sightings of it in his *Vitruvius Scoticus*! Before, we rattle around covering an enormous mileage tediously telling everyone how exhausted we felt. We now do have our large slice of life's cake–our drawing-room is in the one William Adam stateroom which was completed in 1732. It looks south towards the Moorfoots where once the cascade flowed and one feels very cushioned from a world which, in this day and age, at times I cease to understand. In return for so much, all I can promise you is the dedication of Aedrian, my husband, and myself to our home and its future. We have carried out an intensive programme of restoration over the past 18 years. The reason we have not yet reinstated the John Adam drawing-room and dining-room is that dry rot has manifested itself in other parts of the house and finances are stretched. Those past, present and future, who love Arniston should be eternally grateful for the advice of the Historic Buildings' Council to the Government which has resulted in such very generous grant aid for the house, and there is more pending. There have been times of despair over the past eighteen years. The dry rot predator has a habit of striking at one's most unguarded moments. It is then that the encouragement and moral support of friends has been invaluable to us, giving us renewed impetus to carry on.

Sources: Arniston Memoirs xxxxx + family anecdotes.

Arniston House, Midlothian

William Adam's Seal: Palladio, Inigo Jones and the Image of Vitruvius Scoticus

The seals used by William Adam and his sons, intaglios which portray Palladio and Inigo Jones or contain other architectural allusions, are examined for the light they shed on the image the Adam architectural dynasty wished to cultivate as an aid to professional advancement.

FOR John Evelyn and Joseph Addison, writers of classic works on numismatics which greatly influenced the taste of Augustan cognoscenti, medals 'gave light to history'.[1] The two writers might easily have passed the same judgment on the sort of ancient intaglios (or the post-Renaissance gems which were much more common) often used as seals by their own contemporaries. A seal could, in Evelyn's or Addison's phrase, give light to the recipient of a letter: it could be a commentary upon the sender, or afford acknowledged or unacknowledged testimony to his character, his vision of himself, or his aspirations. The choice of a seal showed the writer in the light he considered to suit him best; for seals were frequently employed to convey a message, or as propaganda of a refined and scholarly kind, or to make (in a sense more than the purely literal) an impression. As with antique or pseudo-antique gems, so with devices cut in intaglio to the wishes of a man who sought to use that device to make a point, or to establish a case for appraisal by his correspondents in a particular way. In an age before the anonymity of the adhesive envelope, the seal might hold a significance of a sort conveyed to us most commonly by the corporate logo—and, as we shall see, the 'public relations' element in such a device, even the 'marketing strategy' underlying its use, was not wholly absent. Although it would be easy to be diverted by seals—Sir John Clerk of Penicuik once admitted archly that he had been so taken with a friend's intaglio that he had almost forgotten to open the letter[2]—it cannot be denied that there is information to be had from such sources which will be missed if we fail to pay due attention to these small wax images. The series used by William Adam and his sons is a most interesting case in point. For William Adam used a seal with the head of Inigo Jones upon it; and his successors possessed other seals with architectural allusions. The purpose of this article is to establish the sources of these images, and to discuss the significance of their use by the Adam architectural dynasty.

Publication of Colen Campbell's seminal *Vitruvius Britannicus* provided the model of an album of designs for William Adam to follow. The idea of producing a *Vitruvius Scoticus*—perhaps a more suitable title for an architect who had not, unlike Campbell, chosen to migrate to London in pursuit of patronage on a greater scale than post-Union

Scotland could afford—was apparently conceived about 1726.[3] Initially Adam himself, on his subscription receipt forms, called the projected work by no more elaborate a title than 'Designs for Buildings &c'.[4] It may well have been a friend and patron such as Sir John Clerk, uniquely sensitive to Scotland's equivocal national identity after 1707, or else the poet and bookseller Allan Ramsay, crony of Richard Cooper (the principal engraver of the series of plates which were to make up *Vitruvius Scoticus*) and a man ever watchful for a commercial opportunity even as he was an ardent Scottish patriot, who began to allude to the projected book of designs by the title it now bears.[5] It was first referred to by an observer of the Scottish antiquarian, artistic and architectural scene as 'a Vitruvius Scoticus' in 1733.[6] The idea of imitation or reflection of the *Vitruvius Britannicus* model will have been clear and appealing to all in Adam's Edinburgh circle.

In 1726 Adam planned to go to London to put in hand the engraving of the plates.[7] This trip was postponed until the next year, and even then he made no definite progress with the commissioning of the engraving. He will, however, almost certainly have been able to puff the book among the members of the London Scottish community who were known to patronise native Scottish artists of talent who had set up in the capital, men such as William Aikman in the 1720s, or Allan Ramsay the younger in the next decade. Though members of the Whig establishment, and men who had for reasons of political advancement tended to sublimate their Scottishness into a comprehensive Britishness, these London Scots nevertheless pleased themselves in a harmless and unexceptionable way by promoting the careers of Scottish artists. While they were North Britons in political interest, they could nevertheless, perhaps, take a nationalist artistic pleasure in a work to be called *Vitruvius Scoticus*.

But by about 1740, work on the production of the plates for the projected book seems to have stopped.[8] No book appeared. It is significant that at this very time the Inigo Jones seal came into use by William Adam. Was this, perhaps, some alternative way—very slight, but very subtle—to gain recognition by an intriguing exercise in what we should call public relations work or in image-making? Just as the turning of the mason from Kirkcaldy, the compiler of 'the book of Scotch Houses', into the author of *Vitruvius Scoticus* was all part of the 'packaging' of the architect, so was the adoption of this particularly significant seal an aspect of the overall propaganda exercise. Public relations and image-making were something of which Robert and James Adam, in their turn, were to have a keen understanding. There is nothing more touching, and at the same time revealing, to emerge from a study of the Adam family's use of allusive seals, than to note the letter to Lord Milton in which Robert Adam announced his father's death.[9] In John Adam's absence, Robert (as second son) took up his father's signet; and the moving letter with its Inigo Jones head impressed in the black wax announces not just the passing of the paterfamilias of the Adam dynasty, but seems also to portend the emergence of a new prodigy of architectural genius which, through the early adoption of the Jones talisman, anticipates the advent of its own 'kind of revolution'.

William Adam's seal is derived ultimately from Van Dyck's portrait of Inigo Jones, an image best known in the form of engravings. The prime begetter of the Adam seal is the celebrated drawing by Van Dyck (itself related to the oil painting of which the finest version is now in the Hermitage, Leningrad) which was given by the third Duke of Devonshire to Lord Burlington (Fig. 1). It then passed back by descent to the Chatsworth collection. After this chalk drawing was made the plate by Robert Van Voerst for Van Dyck's *Iconography*.[10]

In the original drawing, and the oils which are related to it, the head faces right. In the engraving by Van Voerst this is, of course, reversed, although Inigo continues to face in the same direction as in the Van Dyck original in the derivitive frontispiece (by Hollar) to Jones's *The Most Notable Antiquity of Great Britain, vulgarly called Stone-Heng. . .Restored*, which work had been prepared for the press by John Webb and published in 1655. The Inigo of the Van Dyckian image is caught, as it were, in mid-sentence of some animated conversation, lips parted, eyes flashing, hair wind-blown where it escapes from beneath a close-fitting skullcap. His buttoned doublet has a broad falling collar. Certain features of the engraved portrait after Van Dyck survive, as we shall see, even to the tiny Adam seal: the collar with its distinctive curl on the right-hand point, the wispy hair to the left of the head. The nine close-set buttons which appear on the doublet in the original portrait are reduced in the Adam seal to seven; but they have by this time acquired distinctive long button-holes. Small fact though this last is, it is nevertheless a pointer to the more immediate ancestry of the Adam seal.

The great-grandparent of the seal is the Van Dyck portrait drawing. The grandparent is Rysbrack's bust of Jones which depended for its source upon the Van Dyck (Fig. 2).[11] This famous image of 'the British Vitruvius' owed its existence to what Margaret Whinney called 'the growing sense of the glory of England's past'.[12] There was a demand in Lord Burlington's circle and among would-be connoisseurs of the 1720s and 1730s for three-dimensional likenesses of the presiding genius of the architectural revolution which we call neo-Palladianism, of which the hero was Inigo Jones. A more austere, not to say sour, critic than Whinney, C.F. Bell, writing in 1937 before the re-evaluation of the British sculptural tradition of the eighteenth century had begun, described the way in which the cult of Inigo Jones had been furnished with suitable votive images as a process akin to the fabrication of 'film-history', to the devotees of which 'liveliness is more convincing than historical truth': for the eighteenth-century equivalents of Bell's vulgar aficionados of the cinema, 'sculptors of the barocco period' had produced acceptable 'animated busts, based on the Vandyck'.[13] Thus was the two-dimensional image of Inigo as conceived by Van Dyck and transmitted by Van Voerst and Hollar translated into the three-dimensional form of busts, reliefs, statuettes and full-size statues. The Jones cult was promoted especially by Lord Burlington, but it was carried on by many a lesser architect and patron.[14] In his use of a seal with Inigo's head (Fig. 3),

1. Sir Anthony Van Dyck: Inigo Jones. Black chalk on white paper, 24.5 × 20 ($9\frac{5}{8}$ × $7\frac{7}{8}$). Trustees of the Chatsworth Settlement; print supplied by Courtauld Institute of Art. This drawing was engraved, in reverse, by Robert Van Voerst and from it is derived the Rysbrack bust.

2. John Michael Rysbrack: Inigo Jones. Marble, 68.6 × 48.6 (27 × 19). Trustees of the Chatsworth Settlement; print supplied by Courtauld Institute of Art. This bust, derived from the Van Dyck image, is the link between contemporary *ad vivum* likenesses of Inigo and the many 18th century three-dimensional portraits of an almost mythical architectual hero.

95)

William Adam was making a statement no less eloquent (albeit scaled down), and in fact rather earlier, than Burlington's, when the architect-earl sat to George Knapton for a portrait in which the Rysbrack bust looms out of the background as some sort of presiding deity.[15] And if Burlington was shown in that portrait holding a volume of Palladio, then, as we shall see, the Adam family did not neglect their own tribute of allusion and respect to the master himself.

A product of the antiquarian patriotism of the day, and a fine example of Rysbrack's ability to capture the idea of an historical personality whom neither he nor his patrons had ever seen in the flesh, his Inigo Jones became the standard image of the architect, 'for truth of Likeness and property of ornaments' (in Vertue's phrase) as if indeed done from the life.[16] Rysbrack's first documented 're-creation' of Jones as a British worthy or national hero in a portrait which carried utter conviction was a commission by Henry Hoare for Stourhead and dates from October 1727.[17] But it was almost certainly Burlington who first obtained from Rysbrack a bust of Inigo. It is possible that Adam and Sir John Clerk saw plaster copies of Burlington's commission when they were in London together in 1727. Clerk, indeed, may well have seen the actual marble bust when he inspected the Earl's works of art and his collections of Palladio and Inigo Jones drawings at Burlington House. On his next visit to London some six years later, Clerk actually visited Rysbrack's studio and workshop, where he recorded having seen 'many bustoes and bass relieves in marble and clay, done with exceeding delicacy.'[18] At any event, the Burlington bust set the fashion for copies and versions, reproductions and reductions, in marble, stone and plaster; for a statue at Chiswick; and for medallions of the architect.[19] Since the Rysbrack bust and its derivatives had been founded upon the engraving after Van Dyck, these face left, and they have an upward tilt to the head.

With medallions and plaques of Inigo Jones we approach more nearly to the type of image that is conveyed by the seal impression: a three-dimensional portrait derived from a two-dimensional drawing or print, yet without the all-round visibility of a free-standing bust or statuette. A medallion portrait of Inigo forms part of the allegorical frontispiece to William Kent's *Designs of Inigo Jones*, which was published in 1727. This is related to the Van Dyck/Rysbrack image, although the collar is rather wider. It is not difficult to imagine the appealing idea of translating such an engraved medallion portrait into a seal. The correspondence between Allan Ramsay (in his role as bookseller and dealer in miscellaneous works of art) and Sir John Clerk informs us that at a date late in the 1720s Clerk acquired from Ramsay not only a copy of Kent's *Jones*, but also a certain ring set with an intaglio.[20] There may of course be no significance in the fact that mention of Clerk's ring is followed immediately by mention of the named book; but what is certain is that Clerk, too, acquired at some time, then or later, a seal bearing a slightly smaller version of the Inigo head. A copy of Kent's *Designs of Inigo Jones* was also in the possession of William Adam.[21] Thus by, say, 1730, both Scotland's leading architect, and her

3. William Adam's seal. An impression in red wax from a letter of William Adam to Lord Milton, 1747. Robert Adam used this seal after his father's death. National Library of Scotland.

4. John Adam's seal, in the later version bearing the inscription DIVINA PALLADIS ARTE. An impression in red wax on a letter of 1758 addressed to Lord Milton. National Library of Scotland.

5. James Adam's seal of Palladio's head, derived from Rysbrack's bust, itself after William Kent's drawing. An impression in black wax on a letter to Lord Milton of 1759. National Library of Scotland.

leading arbiter of taste, were in a position to indulge in the business of paying personal tribute to 'our admired Inigo Jones', as Clerk called him in the notes to 'The Country Seat', his didactic poem on country-house architecture and landscape design.[22] Further evidence for the growth of the Jones cult in Scotland is furnished by another letter from Ramsay to Clerk in which he lists a number of bas-reliefs which he offered to Sir John.[23] These, Ramsay explained, he had had 'lately from abroad'. The list is of plaques of standard classical subjects, of which one example can still be identified in the collection at Penicuik House. A curious interloper in this consignment, however, is a plaque of Inigo Jones, which in its juxtaposition with characters from classical mythology is itself some indication of the growing cult-status of the architect. The probability must be that Ramsay's plaque was also a derivative of the Van Dyck/Rysbrack image. Some years later Wedgwood was producing plaques of Jones, one of which is certainly of this type.[24]

In 1740, which is the date when (as surviving correspondence shows) William Adam began systematically to use his Inigo seal, the medallist John Kirk, then aged only 16, produced his version of the now-standard portrait of Jones.[25] This medal, which is very rare, a few only having been struck as presents to the artist's friends, provides the closest parallel with the Adam seal. The doublet has the nine buttons of the original portrait, but has the addition of long button-holes: the Rysbrack bust has three buttons with holes of medium length. Adam's seal was engraved with seven buttons and long holes. Clerk's has four buttons with long holes. These details serve to indicate that while superficially the same, at least three glyptic portraits of Jones can be distinguished as separate contributions to his iconography, although all descend from a common source.

That it was the head of Inigo Jones that Clerk and Adam chose to have on their seals is testimony of a kind to at least a theoretical adherence to the precepts of the neo-Palladian revolution. As is well known, neither Clerk nor Adam was a thorough-going Palladian in actuality. Yet both were, without doubt, fully aware of Jones's outstanding importance for the subsequent course of British architectural history. They knew their *Vitruvius Britannicus*, and Campbell's praise (as he had expressed it in the Preface to the first volume) of the great progenitors, 'the Renowned Palladio' and 'the Famous Inigo Jones'. May we not legitimately ask whether there is any evidence on the part of Adam and Clerk of some overt participation in the cult of Palladio himself?

As far as Clerk was concerned, this seems to have been confined to a literary acknowledgement only of 'Palladio as master of our admired Inigo Jones', or as an interpreter of the ancient Roman architectural achievement through his drawings of classical buildings. When Palladio is mentioned elsewhere in 'The Country Seat' it is coupled with an injunction to the reader to avoid the folly of too close and impractical an imitation of Venetian villa-planning and design in the North British climate. Clerk appears to stress the importance of munificent and knowledgeable patrons as encouragers and motivators of architectural talent. The United Kingdom of Great Britain provided unmatched opportunities for achievement in all fields, and in architecture as in the amassing of collections of art and antiquities for 'out-Italianising the Italians'.[26] Thus it was to Jones as the man who had naturalised Palladio, rather than to Palladio himself, that he tended to look. William Adam may have shared this view; but his sons saw more clearly the true descent of their art.

John, Robert and James Adam possessed seals which indicate veneration—or the idea of it, at any rate—for Palladio himself. John, as a disciple of the neo-Palladianism of Isaac Ware, used an intaglio with an acanthus-shrouded column capital as its device. Two versions of this seal seem to have been employed at various times: the field, originally blank, came to be occupied by the engraved motto DIVINA PALLADIS ARTE above the capital and foliage (Fig. 4).[27] The source for this tiny emblem appears to be the uppermost feature (i.e. a Corinthian capital overgrown by acanthus fronds) of the ornamental cartouche, drawn by Kent and engraved by Vertue, surrounding the portrait of Palladio which itself is set between Venetian lions flanked by rinceau ornament to form the decorative headpiece to the address to the reader at the opening of Burlington's *Fabbriche Antiche disegnate da Andrea Palladio* of 1730. On occasion Robert also used the capital device without the inscription, and James used a different, rather more elaborate intaglio of the same motif and motto, though not one taken from the same source.[28] This was before Robert and James went to Italy. More interesting by virtue of its affinity with the source of William Adam's Inigo seal is that intaglio which we find James Adam using in 1759 (Fig. 5).[29] His seal bore a head of Palladio which is directly derived from Rysbrack's bust (Fig. 6),[30] of which the source is the plate redrawn by William Kent after an engraved portrait of the Italian. This likeness was in Burlington's possession, and Kent's rendering of it (engraved by Arthur Pond) was to be found as the frontispiece to Burlington's own edition of Palladio's drawings of the ancient baths, the *Fabbriche Antiche* to which reference has already been made. As such, this Adam device is of considerable interest, for it is one of the very few known reproductions or reductions in any medium of the Rysbrack bust.[31] Whether James Adam himself had this seal made, or whether his father ordered it at the time he acquired the Inigo intaglio, must remain a matter of speculation. Its continued use by James in Italy is striking, given his critical attitude to Palladio and his legacy when he actually encountered the work of the master on his home ground. Writing to his mother from Vicenza on 8 October 1760 James arrogantly belittles Palladio as 'one of those fortunate Genius's who has purchas'd reputation at an easy rate'; and there on the back of this very letter is his seal of Palladio's head.[32]

If the album of designs representing the best of Scottish architecture of the age which was taking shape as *Vitruvius Scoticus* can in some ways be seen as an illustrated companion to the theory of country-house design as propounded in the contemporary blank verse dicta of Sir John Clerk's 'The Country Seat', so both Adam the practical architect and Clerk the amateur and arbiter of taste found a common icon in the Inigo seal. Both saw

6. John Michael Rysbrack: Andrea Palladio. Marble, 59.7 × 45.7 (23½ × 18). Trustees of the Chatsworth Settlement; print supplied by Courtauld Institute of Art. This was the classic image of Palladio as the neo-Palladians liked to imagine him.

themselves as promoters of Scottish architectural achievement in the practical and theoretical realms. There should be no shame in the overt Scottishness of the title of Adam's proposed book. That he and Clerk were North Britons was not in doubt: Clerk was a Baron of the Court of Exchequer, Adam a Government contractor. They chose simply to add a Scottish dimension to the grand procession of British architecture, to make a virtue of separateness within the general cultural tradition of international classicism. By using the evocative image of the Inigo Jones seal they were acknowledging their fealty to that tradition, and to the precept of Pope as expressed to Lord Burlington, that he and all British architects and patrons should endeavour

> Jones and Palladio to themselves restore
> And be whate're Vitruvius was before.[33]

National Library of Scotland

NOTES AND REFERENCES

After this paper had been written, I discovered by chance that Mr Malcolm Baker of the Department of Sculpture of the Victoria and Albert Museum had also, quite independently, been working on a related, but rather wider, topic. His article 'Portrait Busts of Architects in Eighteenth-Century Britain' relates to mine in that we are both to some extent concerned with matters involving the changing status of the architect as a professional, and with the way in which architects perceived and presented themselves. Baker discusses these issues in the context of portrait busts. He shows that the demand for portrait busts–though there were, in fact, very few of these–grows at a time when the status of the architect was rising; and he suggests very cogently that, by having such images of themselves, architects were claiming a certain social status. The fact, for example, that there is a marble bust of William Adam, perhaps by Henry Cheere, says much for his standing and for the Adam family's 'sense of their own status'. To commission a bust was to make a claim about one's social standing, and it was to emulate the customs of those of higher rank. A bust provided an 'image of politeness'. In very similar vein, I have argued in my own paper that the use of the Inigo Jones and other seals was a matter of image-making. These two articles, therefore, produced separately and coincidentally, complement each other. I am very grateful to Mr Baker for letting me read the text of his paper, which will appear in C. Hind, ed., *New Light on English Neo-Palladianism, London, 1990.*

1. John Evelyn, *Numismata. A Discourse of Medals, Antient and Modern* London, 1697, p. 250; Joseph Addison, *Dialogues upon the Usefulness of Ancient Medals, especially in relation to the Latin and Greek Poets*, Glasgow, 1751, p. 8.

2. National Library of Scotland, MS. 3044, fol. 87, Clerk to Robert Arbuthnott, 22 February 1726.

3. William Adam, *Vitruvius Scoticus*, edited and with an introduction by James Simpson, Edinburgh, 1980, Introduction, p. 6.

4. John Fleming, *Robert Adam and his Circle in Edinburgh and Rome*, London, 1962, p. 48.

5. On Clerk, Ramsay and Scottish national sentiment of this circle and period see Iain Gordon Brown, 'Modern Rome and Ancient Caledonia: the Union and the politics of Scottish culture', in Andrew Hook, ed., *The History of Scottish Literature*, vol. ii, Aberdeen, 1987, Chapter 2, passim. On Ramsay's relations with Richard Cooper see Iain Gordon Brown, *Poet and Painter: Allan Ramsay, father and son, 1684–1784*, Edinburgh, 1984, p. 10.

6. Howard Colvin, *Biographical Dictionary of British Architects*, London, 1978, p. 56, n.

7. John Gifford, *William Adam 1689–1748. A Life and Times of Scotland's Universal Architect*, Edinburgh, 1989, pp. 107–8.

8. *Vitruvius Scoticus*, ed. Simpson, Introduction, p. 7.

9. NLS, MS. 16655, fol. 15, 25 June 1748.

10. Marie Mauquoy-Hendrickx, *L'Iconographie d'Antoine Van Dyck. Catalogue raisonné*, Brussels, 1956, p. 235, no. 72; David Piper, *Catalogue of 17th century Portraits in the National Portrait Gallery*, Cambridge, 1963, pp. 182–3; John Harris, Stephen Orgel and Roy Strong, *The King's Arcadia: Inigo Jones and the Stuart Court*, London, 1973, pp. 212–3; Oliver Millar, *Van Dyck in England*, London, 1982, p. 111–2.

11. M.I. Webb, *Michael Rysbrack, Sculptor*, London, 1954, p. 102. See also Malcolm Baker's catalogue entry for number 144 in *The Treasure Houses of Britain: Five Hundred Years of Private Patronage and Art collecting*, edited by Gervase Jackson-Stops, New Haven and London, 1985.

12. Margaret Whinney, *Sculpture in Britain 1530–1830*, second edition, Harmondsworth, 1988, p. 169.

13. C.F. Bell, 'Portraits of Inigo Jones', *Journal of the Royal Institute of British Architects*, third series, XLIV, 1936–7, p. 1008.

14. In course of discussion of William Adam's seal it should be noted that one other case of a man connected with the eighteenth-century building world owning an Inigo signet is documented. Joseph Sanderson's will mentions his 'gold ring of Inigo Jones's head'. I am grateful to Mr Malcolm Baker for bringing this reference (which occurs in Colvin's *Biographical Dictionary*, p. 717) to my attention.

15. On the Knapton portrait see F. Saxl and R. Wittkower, *British Art and the Mediterranean*, new edition, London, 1969, section 53; [John Wilton-Ely] *Apollo of the Arts: Lord Burlington and his Circle*, Nottingham, 1973, p. 24; and Francis Russell's entry for number 139 in the exhibition catalogue *The Treasure Houses of Britain*. Wittkower decided that the book in question was a Palladio. Wilton-Ely and Russell have stated that it is a volume of Kent's *Designs of Inigo Jones*. It is surely too small in format to

be the latter. My own feeling is that, if it is not intended simply as just the idea of a book, doubtless one of implied architectural significance, then it is Giacomo Leoni's or, more probably on grounds of size, Colen Campbell's or Isaac Ware's editions of Palladio, the one sponsored by Burlington and the other dedicated to him. If that is so, then Burlington, in this portrait, has the satisfaction of paying homage to both his architectural heroes at once, and not solely to Jones through two separate allusive studio props.

16. cf. Katharine Eustace, *Michael Rysbrack*, Bristol, 1982, p. 14; *Vertue Notebooks*, III, Walpole Society, vol xxii, p. 84.

17. M.I. Webb, 'Sculpture by Rysbrack at Stourhead', *Burlington Magazine*, XCII, 1950, p. 311.

18. Scottish Record Office, Clerk of Penicuik Muniments, GD 18/2107, p. 39. ('A Journey to London, 1727'); GD 18/2110/1, p. 25 ('A Toure into England in the year 1733').

19. Webb, *Rysbrack*, pp. 101, 102, 109; John Physick, *Designs for English Sculpture, 1680–1860*, London, 1969, pp. 78–9; Baker in *The Treasure Houses of Britain* exhibition catalogue, number 144.

20. *The Works of Allan Ramsay*, edited by A.M. Kinghorn and A. Law, Scottish Text Society, fourth series, vi, Edinburgh, 1970, IV, Letter 25.

21. *Blair Adam Library. Catalogue*, London, 1883, p. 40.

22. 'The Country Seat', SRO, GD 18/4404/1, note 7.

23. *Works of Allan Ramsay*, IV, Letter 52; Iain Gordon Brown, ''Plaister Gimcracks'': the handicraft of Allan Ramsay the poet', *Review of Scottish Culture*, II, 1986, pp. 19–22.

24. Robin Reilly and George Savage, *Wedgwood: the Portrait Medallions*, London, 1973, p. 200.

25. See Edward Hawkins, *Medallic Illustrations of the History of Great Britain and Ireland to the death of George III*, edited by A.W. Franks and H.A. Greuber, vol. i, London, 1885, p. 398, no. 25; cf. R.J. Eidlitz, *Medals and Medallions relating to Architects from the Collection of Robert James Eidlitz*, New York, 1927, no. 609 and plate 68.

26. SRO, GD 18/4404/1, notes 5, 7, 8.

27. E.g., NLS, MS. 16690, fols. 2–3.

28. SRO, GD 18/4744, 11 Aug 1754.

29. E.g., NLS, MS. 16708, fol. 8.

30. On the Palladio bust see Webb, *Rysbrack*, pp. 102–3; Wilton-Ely, *Apollo of the Arts*, p. 45.

31. On the scarcity of reproductions and reductions of the Rysbrack Palladio, see Baker's catalogue entry for number 143 in *The Treasure Houses of Britain*; and the same author's essay 'Portrait Busts of Architects in Eighteenth-Century Britain' referred to at the head of these notes.

32. SRO, GD 18/4875, 8 Oct 1760.

33. 'Moral Essays: Epistle IV', lines 193–4.

Mavisbank: The story since 1973

This is the story of the public endeavours since the 1973 fire to restore Mavisbank—designed by William Adam and built by Sir John Clerk in 1720–25—a building of European significance, of great historical impor-tance and of outstanding beauty situated in the Esk Valley below Loanhead, ten miles from the centre of Edinburgh.

THE SCENE

In December 1973 the centre block of Mavisbank, already damaged by mining subsi-dence, was destroyed by fire. It was under-insured and only £6000 was paid to the owner, Mrs A.C.B. Stevenson. Mr Archie Stevenson, by then estranged from his wife, took to living in a caravan in the forecourt and by October 1977 there were eleven caravans or chassis and thirty-three old cars in front of the house. A dramatic picture was published in the *Times*. In 1978 the policies, amounting to some seventy acres, were sold to Mrs Martin, one of the three daughters who lived in America, and the house and the two pavilions were sold separately to three Americans. Mr Stevenson retains the life rent and has authority to act for the owners.

The Scottish Georgians

The Scottish Georgian Society under its Chairman, Colin McWilliam, called the first meeting on 20th May 1975 and the Society and Midlothian District Council commis-sioned the first technical report from Ove Arup explaining the subsistence damage. It was circulated with a report by James Simpson in June 1976 suggesting that in view of its importance both house and policies should be designated as a Conservation area. This was approved by Midlothian on 10th November 1977 and was accepted as being of outstanding value by the Historic Buildings Council for Scotland on 1st March 1978.

The Midlothian District Council is Local Planning Authority

On 24th February 1978 Midlothian District Council served to secure the removal of the caravans and clearance of the cars which were without planning consent under Sections 84 and 63 of the Town and Country Planning (Scotland) Act 1972. Although Mr Stevenson's appeal against these Notices was dismissed by the Secretary of State on 19 November 1979, there were further legal representations ending up in the House of Lords, and it was not until October 1985 that the forecourt was cleared by contractors sent in by the Midlothian District Council. It is reported that this enforcement action cost Midlothian some £30 000.

Midlothian as Buildings Authority

On 28 February 1978 Midlothian District Council also served a Section 13 Notice under the Building (Scotland) Act 1959 requiring the owner either to carry out repair works or to demolish the House. As a result of strong objections from the Scottish Georgian Society, the Scottish Civic Trust and the Lothian Regional Council, the Secretary of State only approved the repair works and not the demolition of the house on 10 March 1978.

The Lothian Regional Council

The Lothian Regional Council, which had been set up on the reorganisation of local government in May 1975, had taken an interest in Mavisbank pursuivant on its structure plan policy para 68 which stated: 'Among the glories of Lothian are the fine country estates which combine architecture and landscape art. The Regional Council believes that the heritage of these estates should be preserved and their value to the community enhanced'.

They had commissioned a further report from Ove Arup produced in January 1978 specifying the works necessary for the stabilisation of the buildings at a cost of £16 200 and in February 1978, after a visit, decided to pay for the stabilisation on condition that they could acquire the whole estate. However, it was finally accepted in February 1981 that Mr Stevenson was not prepared to sell by agreement to the Lothian Regional Council.

The Secretary of State

The Regional Council had not the powers to serve Listed Building Repair notices under Section 105 leading to Compulsory Purchase, under Section 104, of the Town and Country Planning (Scotland) Act 1972. Midlothian District Council had declined to follow up their Section 105 Notices of March 1977 with a Compulsory Purchase Order in June 1978 but made representations that the Secretary of State, who had these powers, should exercise them.

The Lothian Regional Council also pressed the Secretary of State to use these powers and obtained an undertaking from the National Heritage Memorial Fund that they would give substantial assistance to Lothian Regional Council towards the purchase price in order to reimburse the Secretary for State, but getting round the limitations on capital investment at that time.

The Lothian Building Preservation Trust

In July 1985 Midlothian Director of Planning, Bob Maslin, asked the Director of the newly established Lothian Preservation Trust, Frank Tindall, who had retired from the post of Director of Physical Planning at the Lothian Region, to end the inactivity by direct action. The Trust agreed that it would undertake to restore Mavisbank if adequately funded and proceed in December 1985 to get a valuation of £95 200 for the estate, but this was not acceptable to Mr Stevenson.

Coal Mining

In November 1985 the National Coal Board announced its intention of extracting coal under Mavisbank. As a result of representations by the Lothian Building Preservation Trust and the Architectural Heritage Society for Scotland (as the Scottish Georgian Society had renamed itself) the Scottish Development Department agreed to commission Baptie Geo-Technical to report on the effect of the mining on Mavisbank and advise measures to protect it. An interim report was produced in March 1986 and a final report after four boreholes were drilled in August 1986. These confirmed that the ground under Mavisbank was stable ('what else would one expect of a William Adam building?') and so restoration was not ruled out. Coal mining was however beginning to cause further structural deterioration and the Scottish Development warned the owners that they intended to serve a Section 97 Notice under the Town and Country Planning (Scotland) Act 1972 requiring urgent repairs to the building costing some £16 500.

The Dramatic Events of 26 March 1987

Midlothian District Council decided on 23 March 1987 that in view of the danger they would have to send in the demolition contractors at three days' notice. The Scottish Development Department could not persuade the Council to allow time for them to serve their statutory notice, and the demolition machine moved in.

The Lothian Building Preservation Trust, who had always kept in touch with Archie Stevenson and were in fact negotiating for the House and ten acres, decided that they had just enough legal status to serve an interdict on Midlothian District Council. This was granted at 11·45 pm on 26 March 1987 by Lord Kirkwood. Earlier that day the Trust had obtained competitive tenders for a security fence round the House. This was pegged out and started at 3 pm but Lord Kirkwood required a twenty-four hour guard in addition. So the Trust organised a Volunteer Watch, some thirty strong, which guarded the House for eighteen days until the Scottish Development Department could get the Section 97 Notice duly served. Thus Mavisbank was saved from demolition. Everyone was powerless to act except the Trust.

Subsequently the Scottish Development Department, Historic Buildings and Monuments Directorate served a second Section 97 order and carried out further works, costing £69 000, to consolidate the building and brace it with scaffolding poles. Bilston Glen Colliery closed in May 1989 before causing any further damage and so the building remains today.

The Trust's Feasibility Study

The Trust then decided to produce a feasibility study to prove that it was practical and to establish the costs of restoring Mavisbank. They commissioned James Simpson to prepare plans for its restoration as a single house, Jimmy Wren to determine the structure, Jim Lennie the costs for the buildings and Mark Turnbull the costs for the landscape—£3 000 000 in all, with a value of £750 000 for the finished house and grounds. The 54-page report was written by the Trust's director and circulated widely in April 1989.

The Trust followed this up by a large meeting in the Signet Library under the chairmanship of Lord Bute to prove that it was in the national interest to restore Mavisbank. This meeting passed a unanimous resolution 'calling on the Government to take the leading role in the acquisition of Mavisbank House and its policies with a view to its restoration on the lines proposed in the Trust's Feasibility Study'.

Scottish Office

It is good to report that at the William Adam Tercentenary Conference at Hopetoun House on 28 October 1989 Lord James Douglas Hamilton, MP, Environment Minister at the Scottish Office announced 'that the Government fully share the view that the continued inaction can only lead to the loss of the house and that a building of the importance deserves special consideration. So to break the impasse and to help remove continuing uncertainty about its future the Secretary of State has now decided to look at the possibility of taking Mavisbank into State care so that it can be protected while considerations is given to its future. The Government recognises that Mavisbank deserves a far better fate than death by neglect.'

The Lothian Building Preservation Trust has therefore brought its four year campaign, which has cost some £16 000, to a successful conclusion. It remains ready to assume responsibility for the restoration of Mavisbank if adequately funded.

Ford House, Midlothian
15 December 1989

An Appreciation

COLIN McWilliam died suddenly last December and left us all deprived of his wisdom, but secure in the knowledge that he had taught us all, the professional and the man in the street, how to take a critical look at buildings, think about them, and enjoy the good and the inferior, which only Colin could describe in words with such a wealth and richness of meaning.

Colin McWilliam arrived in Edinburgh late in 1951 on a six-month engagement as a draughtsman in the Scottish National Buildings Record. He was 'found' in the British School in Rome by the then Honorary Secretary of the Record, A.E. Haswell Miller, Keeper of the Scottish National Portrait Gallery, and offered the job, but still had one obstacle to get past–a meeting with Ian G. Lindsay and Sir Frank Mears, who were delegated to interview him. He passed with flying colours. Who in Scotland had heard of architectural history? Certainly not the part-time assistant waiting trembling to greet him. We got down to business, straight out to Mid Calder Parish Church and up the scaffolding, the inspection producing one of Colin's inimitable plans, and instructions to stop worrying about insurance. Colin was interested in the whole range of architecture but found his visual approach satisfied particularly by the Victorian period, so much so that we recorded Burn and Bryce buildings from the beginning, and accepted with open hands the gift of the William Burn office drawings from the RIBA Drawings Collection, a gift now much regretted by the RIBA. He created a climate of interest in Scotland in Victorian buildings and in late 1952, finding a kindred spirit in David Walker's enthusiasm, influenced Ian G. Lindsay, I am confident, in his position as Chief Adviser to the Department of Health for Scotland, to list Victorian and later buildings years in advance of England.

Today in the National Monuments Record of Scotland we still consider Colin's definition of a record of a building as the most appropriate. He defined it in three ways; a document for the purpose of repair or reconstruction, one which provides an experience as near as possible to that of visiting the building itself, and a means by which the building may be studied in relation to other buildings, its history, type, date and architect. Such a record can be used for many different purposes.

Colin became an assistant Secretary with the National Trust for Scotland in 1957, and carried his enthusiasm for the aesthetic assessment of buildings and their surroundings to his presentation of their guide leaflets. Culzean Castle springs to mind in particular, where Adam's romantic conception 'the castle on the cliff' was shown by Colin in relation to the designed landscape and garden buildings, where prospects occur by chance, or were designed to make an impact. In an urban environment his eye caught the charm of the mixture of vernacular and designed buildings. His book *Scottish Townscape* published in 1975 was ahead of its time, and gave us glimpses of the later inspired writing in the Lothian and Edinburgh volumes of the *Buildings of Scotland* series, in which his witty, sometimes playful, but always compassionate look at buildings will be read and enjoyed for years to come.

In 1964 Colin was appointed lecturer in the history of architecture at Heriot Watt University based in the College of Art. He brought all his skills, learning and humanism to his work with his students, both in college and at home, where, with his wife Christine, he entertained with flair. In his post-graduate course in architectural conservation, he instilled in his students not only a love of buildings but also his own particular attitude to conservation, which he saw as the consolidation and protection of the original fabric of a building in its relationship with the 'whole place', a prelude to group listing and the setting up of conservation areas. Colin brought this interest and experience to his work with the Scottish Georgian Society, now the Architectural Heritage Society of Scotland. The Society owes a great debt to Colin McWilliam from the beginning, when he and Eleanor Robertson fought to save George Square from University development, and the high standard of comment from the Society's Cases Panels today owes everything to Colin's high standards of informed comment and his continuing courtesy in battle.

Colin fought against the idea that the only proper monument is a dead one. It is a tribute to him that so many of his graduates now work to a very high standard to achieve excellence in the field of historic building conservation in Scotland, bringing use and life to so many historic buildings which would have been considered beyond hope in the past.

Kitty Cruft
National Monuments Record of Scotland

COLIN McWilliam provided a fast-changing firework display which illuminated Scottish architecture. Surprises were frequent, a sense of style always present. His methods were many—literary (the volumes of *The Buildings of Scotland*, *Scottish Townscape*), administrative (Curator of the Scottish National Buildings Record for six years, and Assistant Secretary of the National Trust for Scotland for seven), propaganda (journalist, lecturer and exhibition designer), and educational (twenty-five years at Edinburgh College of Art in charge of architectural history and the post-graduate conservation course). He helped found new organisations—the Stenhouse Conservation Centre, the Edinburgh Antiques and Fine Arts Society, the Scottish Georgian Society of which he was the first Secretary and later Chairman (now the Architectural Heritage Society of Scotland), and the Edinburgh New Town Conservation Committee. He gave energy to those such as the Cockburn Association whose existence pre-dated his, the Scottish Development Agency's Conservation Bureau, and particularly through his links with England at COTAC, ICOMOS and the Victorian Society. In each role he was a fighter—for individual buildings, for the proper performance of church music, for historical scholarship, for worthwhile new architecture, and for the careful and thoughtful conservation of the past. His appreciation of quirks and oddities, both architectural and human, gave him a sympathy for the second- and even third-rate seldom found in those who study, teach and claim to enjoy architecture.

Colin's family and friends have decided to continue his work by setting up a Memorial Fund to support a project in which his memory can find tangible expression. Edinburgh's former Glasite Meeting House at 33 Barony Street is a distinctive but little known New Town building designed by Alexander Black in 1836 and hardly altered since David Bryce replaced the pulpit in 1873. The last members of the congregation have just given it to the Cockburn Conservation Trust to be used as a new headquarters for the Architectural Heritage Society. They will use the former caretaker's flat for their offices, the meeting hall itself will become a lecture theatre, the setting for a regular memorial lecture endowed by the Fund, and the first floor Feast Room where the Glasites lunched between services will be restored as the McWilliam Room for committee meetings, seminars, feasts and perhaps an architectural conservation library.

The Fund is administered by the Royal Incorporation of Architects in Scotland of which Colin was an Honorary Fellow, as he was also of the RIBA—the only person ever to have received this double accolade.

Contributions should be sent to:

RIAS, The Colin McWiliam Memorial Fund,
15 Rutland Square, Edinburgh EH1 2BE

J. Gifford, William Adam 1689–1748–A Life and Times of
Scotland's Universal Architect, *Mainstream, Edinburgh, 1989.*
Paperback, £12.95.

1989 has been a marvellous year for William Adam. His 300th birthday service at
Hamilton parish church, the splendid Exhibition in the National Portrait Gallery, the
AHSS Conference at Hopetoun; these were followed by the promise of work on his
mausoleum in Greyfriars' churchyard, and the statement in John Gifford's book that
'Mavisbank will now survive'. Or was it a command? Anyway the Secretary of State had
no option, after this, but to say that he might be able to buy it, if the price was
reasonable.

The book begins with a look at Scotland's economically backward state before the
Union and indeed for some time after it. Next it considers building materials and skills,
and the beginning of classical architecture for George Heriot's Hospital. Then Adam
himself is the centrepiece; his father John being a mason, his mother Helen being a
daughter of Lord Cranstoun who had been a royalist in the civil wars. He had a good
education at Kirkcaldy Grammar School, trained as a mason, and some time before 1720
paid a visit to the Low Countries whose apparent results were the first home-produced
barley for Scots broth and pantiles for Scots buildings.

In 1716 William Adam married the daughter of his business partner, Mary Robertson.
Their portraits, painted a good deal later, are surely characteristic; hers by Allan Ramsay
with firm mouth and humorous eyes, an excellent architect's wife, and mother to their
ten children; his by William Aikman, every inch the professional man.

The next chapter is mainly about patronage. Adam provided the services of contractor, supplier and gentleman architect, as many as possible and in whatever order. He was
the ultimate package dealer, and his position as Scotland's 'universal architect' having
once been established, he set himself to 'Housing the Great and Good' (another chapter,
and much the longest, alluding to the aristocracy and public servants or *vice versa*) in
suitable but extraordinarily varied style. He was a man to humour his patrons, all of
whom stand revealed in their buildings. 'Graceful, independent and engaging'; everyone
knew where they were with him except Lord Braco, who thought he had cheated him
over Duff House. Adam sued, and won, the case coming before Lord Milton whose house
at Brunstane had been remodelled–by Adam.

And so to a brief consideration of his public buildings (the few surviving must be
treasured) and his record as an owner of houses himself. This is an unusual book, because
there it ends. There is no speculation on how William Adam learned his job as a classical
architect; no 'evaluation' of his international rating, except the fascinating information
that in 1724 Lord Polwarth considered Mr Campbell and Mr Gibbs and then decided on
Adam, though his plans for Redbraes were never carried out. The value-judgements are
all those of Adam's contemporaries.

It is a beautifully produced book (except for a few typographical quirks), though hardly an easy read. But persevere; there are few sentences that do not lead to some further insight. As a teacher of architectural history, I am grateful to John Gifford on my own and my students' behalf for not supplying facile or half-baked opinions. One can reach one's own views and note them in the copious margins.

Colin McWilliam
(This review was written shortly before his
sudden and untimely death on 8 December 1989)

Frank Worsdall, The Glasgow Tenement: A Way of Life
A Social, Historical and Architectural Study, *Richard Drew
Publishing, Glasgow, 165 pp, 1989, £6.99.*

Readers should not expect something new. *The Glasgow Tenement* is a paperback edition of *The Tenement—a Way of Life,* first published by Chambers in 1979. True, it is better value and more attractively packaged than the original and there are changes, like the new title and a glossy cover, which are a great improvement; but these are presentational differences. The content remains virtually the same.

One might have expected a more thorough updating after an energetic decade of rescuing the Glasgow tenement and with it the reputation of the City. A metamorphosis was well under way in the seventies in Glasgow, but change has become much more visible in the eighties. Whole areas of tenements in Dennistoun, Govan, Govanhill, Partick, Woodlands, and elsewhere have been lovingly restored to their original honeys and pinks to become usable homes once again with a certain future. More remarkable is that this has happened largely out of community initiative, itself forcing one of the most profound shifts in housing policy ever witnessed in the United Kingdom. Entire tenement communities have been rescued from otherwise certain municipalisation by this process. None of this is mentioned in the text.

Not everyone will agree with Frank Worsdall's definition of a tenement. Many will recoil at the thought of a multi being called a tenement, or recognise the red tiled two storey buildings on the cover as such.

Worsdall's bias in favour of the tenement is barely concealed. He reflects with nostalgia on a great and glorious past long gone of tight-knit communities, when streets were jammed with people spilling out from their single-ends and room-and-kitchens. In contrast, walking round many familiar parts of Glasgow today can be an unnerving experience. The streets are strangely empty. Often where the buildings survive the vitality has gone.

For all that *The Glasgow Tenement*, alias *The Tenement—A Way of Life*, remains an attractive package. It is still a readable general account in which Frank Worsdall gives

us a delightful glimpse of the Glasgow tenement as he saw it about 15 years ago. It is a personal view reflecting his own interests in Greek Thomson and the City Improvement Trust. He has a keen eye for detail and many of the photographs are his own. It remains one of the few records of a form of building that has dictated the scale and character of all four Scottish cities and many burghs, perhaps because the tenement is so much a part of an urban past that many Scots choose to ignore.

Peter Robinson

William Buchanan, editor, Mackintosh's Masterwork: The Glasgow School of Art, *Richard Drew, Glasgow, 1989. Hardback. £25.00.*

A book like this must operate at two levels: first, descriptive; second, interpretative. And, of course, it does. But how well? Six authors contribute; three—William Buchanan, James Macaulay and Andrew MacMillan—interpret. But how comprehensively? How perceptively?

Buchanan has two essays, one of which sketches in the personalities and events of the art scene centred on The School of Art in *fin-de-siècle* Glasgow, the other describing in some detail the commissioning and construction of Mackintosh's new building. Both are informative, the latter, which constitutes the opening chapter, revealing much about the financial endeavours of the Governors and the preparation of the brief by the Director, Francis Newbery. For the first time the 1896 conditions which applied in the 'Limited Competition of Architects for the Proposed New School of Art' are published. These show clearly that 'The options were very constrained'; Mackintosh evidently provided exactly the accommodation that was required—a factor which perhaps persuaded some of the more conservative Governors to accept his otherwise unexpected architecture.

The book displays this architecture lavishly devoting over a quarter of the text to 'A Tour of the School'. Mackintosh's own drawings are beautifully reproduced, their qualities ironically enhanced by the redundant inclusion of some technically very poor computer projections. There are many lovely photographs not only of the building itself and its endlessly delighting details—it is particularly interesting to study the early interiors by Annan and Bedford Lemere, many reproduced here in sepia, alongside more recent colour views—but of the personalities of its story and of 'The Mackintosh Inheritance' of furniture, paintings, drawings, etc., now housed at the school. But the pages are saturated with this display and the graphic design incontinent, reaching an over indulgent nadir in what can only be described as fly sheet flash.

Alongside such exhaustive description, verbal and visual, the book advances critical comment. James Macaulay contributes a brief essay dealing with those trends in nine-teenth-century architecture concerned with 'Rejecting Overt Historicism'. The stress appears to be on Glasgow; Thomson and, surprisingly beneath such a title, Honeyman, receive attention, but their influence on Mackintosh and the School of Art cannot be demonstrated. Casting the net wider, Macaulay adduces the formal qualities of Scottish Architecture; but a mere two paragraphs seem dismissively inadequate, especially when it is only the baronial and not the vernacular tradition which is invoked. Ultimately, of course, as Macaulay rightly concludes, it is Pugin, Ruskin, Shaw and Voysey who provide the theoretical antecedents (and, in the case of the last two, some of the formal characteristics) of much of Mackintosh's creative work. Sound as this conclusion is, it does seem to vitiate the relevance of the Glaswegian emphasis which introduces this somewhat unfocused chapter.

Andrew MacMillan, too, talks about influence in his essay. He, too, proposes Glasgow, 'Scottish picturesque forms' and the English Free Style movement, adding Japan for exotic but certainly pertinent good measure. But to suggest that Mackintosh was in any sense a proponent of Victorian Glasgow's 'state-of-the-art technology' and that it was this which distinguished him from his English contemporaries is to overstate the case for Mackintosh's Modernism and runs counter to his Ruskinian addiction to architecture as solid mass and his clear expressed disavowal of the 'rose-tinted hallucinations' of Crystal Palace engineering architecture. A hi-tech Mackintosh is scarcely credible.

So, too, to play down the Scottish element in Mackintosh's work—so evident, for example, in the east and south elevations of the School of Art—is to ignore both the built and, again, the written evidence. Why, either then or now, should a concern for cultural context and continuity lead, as MacMillan seems to suggest, to a 'historicist cul-de-sac'? Was it not, in fact, such a pursuit which enabled Mackintosh to uncover a language of form at once functional and symbolic?

Indeed, it was just this discovery, rooted but revolutionary, which made it possible for Mackintosh to make what MacMillan calls his 'major contribution to mainstream modern architecture' (while avoiding the deracinated extremes of any International Style), and it was this same discovery which yet produced those 'iconic images of great potency', part programmatic, part emblematic, images which now evoke a heightened response in the post-modern conscience. To have held these complementary achievements in balance is the delicate nature of Mackintosh's genius. MacMillan sees this well—the title of his essay which describes the School of Art as 'a Modern Enigma' makes this clear—yet his critical path is too confident, on every issue a little too judgmentally positive. For is not the equivocal assessment—now Modernist, now Post-Modernist—bound to entail a more tragic view of the architect?

Mackintosh's is a fragile genius, the measure of which is not to be marked out by the dead hand of time, however richly emblazoned in some historical hall of fame alongside Modernist heroes like Gropius or Mies van der Rohe but, rather, to be forever unfolding in the critical present with self-renewing reticent relevance. If, in its form and content, this book had been less fulsome it would have done Mackintosh and his masterwork greater honour.

Frank Arneil Walker, University of Strathclyde

William Adam Tercentenary Exhibition: Summer 1989

One of the highlights of the tercentenary celebrations was undoubtedly the exhibition on Adam's life and work in the ground floor space of the Scottish National Portrait Gallery. From industrial concerns to the design of major country houses, the complicated story of Adam's varied professional activities and the web of patronage within which he operated was clearly and imaginatively told. Despite the relatively small space available, there were no major omissions that this reviewer could find, although part of the price for this was a slight breakdown in the clarity of organisation in one or two places.

One of the main problems with architectural exhibitions is caused by the difficulty of conveying the character of buildings that really should be visited to be appreciated. Photographs, drawings and prints, particularly of plans can prove rather daunting, not to say boring, to many visitors who have no particular knowledge of architecture. One of the great achievements of this exhibition was the avoidance of this problem through the judicious choice of exhibits and the overall organisation and design of the gallery. The space was divided longitudinally by a mock up of the screen wall of Chatelherault, Adam's spectacular termination to the south avenue at Hamilton Palace, with bays at right angles to it on either side. One very effective device here was the opening up of two of the bull's eye motifs in the screen wall so that the two sides of the exhibition were visually linked. One vista was created between the model of Mavisbank and the model of the House of Dun (situated, appropriately enough, in the section of the exhibition dealing with landscape). Another glimpse through the screen wall, right at the beginning of the exhibition, made a link between the section dealing with the Scottish architectural background and a superb model of Duff House at the very end of the exhibition. Whatever else this was meant to convey, it certainly must have suggested to anyone who, having given the engravings and drawings of the first section a cursory glance, was thinking of retreating to the visually more stimulating material in the *Patrons and Painters* exhibition (to which his ticket also gave him access), that this exhibition contained many good things and was well worth persevering with. Throughout the exhibition there was a lively combination of drawings and engravings; paintings; documents; artefacts, like a masons's tools and a section of a sash window and, most impressive of all, models of several of Adam's most important buildings which, for me, were the outstanding feature of the whole event.

The two main figures in the first section were Sir William Bruce of Kinross and James

Smith. Bruce, recognised by no less a person than Sir John Clerk of Penicuik as 'the chief Introducer of Architecture in this century', was represented mainly by his own house at Kinross and by Holyrood Palace but not, perhaps surprisingly, by Hopetoun House, which was later completely remodelled by Adam. Smith's importance is increasingly being recognised and among his very distinctive drawings were several Italianate designs that look forward to the development of English Palladianism of the early eighteenth century. Smith's style of architecture formed an important element in Adam's life since the family home, Gladney House in Kirkcaldy (the first model in the exhibition), whether built by Adam or someone else, shows clear signs of Smith's influence in the arrangement of the pediment and orders on the façade.

The first half of the exhibition culminated in the great houses of the 1720s, Mavisbank, Arniston and, most notably Hopetoun. There were excellent models of the first two but none of the latter. Perhaps a compensation for this was that it allowed Adam's superb design for the landscape at Hopetoun to provide the main focus of this part of the exhibition. This provided the first of several surprises, if only because of its sheer size which made close examination of much of the detail possible. The elements that make up this garden, the great vistas, the waterworks and parterres, are generally recognised as deriving from the original garden lay-out by Sir William Bruce and Alexander Edward of around 1700 and Adam's drawing fulfills the useful function of suggesting what the original design looked like. This sympathy with an existing formal lay-out also appears to have been a feature of his 'Great Plan' drawn up for the fifth Duke of Hamilton in 1728. This is now lost but other evidence suggests that it was closely based on the surviving 1708 plan by Alexander Edward and even that he may have executed some of Edward's plan.

The exhibition also deals with William Adam as a builder, as opposed to an architect, and an entrepreneur. Adam did not simply design buildings and leave their construction to contractors, but often acted as contractor as well. He was deeply involved in the supply side of the construction industry with his famous brick and tile works at Linktown, Kirkcaldy, yards at Leith with everything from marble to timber and quarries at Queensberry in which freestone could be cut, dressed and even carved before being despatched to sites all over Scotland. There was, however, another side to Adam's entrepreneurial activity which was covered by the exhibition and is also dealt with in some detail by William Kay in his article in this journal. This is Adam's interests in industrial ventures including barley mills, salt pans and coal works which were re-presented by a number of fascinating documents and illustrative material. One minor quibble here is that, although the exhibition did provide us with a very complete picture of Adam's activities from industrial entrepreneur to designer of country houses, it did not clearly bring out the connection between these activities. It was sometimes the case that the architectural improvements on an estate depended on improved income from an activity like coal mining. Hamilton provides us with a good example. Between 1727 and 1743 Adam was involved in a whole series of ambitious projects for the fifth Duke of Hamilton, though most of them were never fully realised. These included the building of Chatelherault and the new parish kirk in Hamilton, redesigning the gardens and surrounding policies as well as work on the palace and on the Duke's apartments at Holyrood palace. However, he also advised on the Duke's coal works at Kinneil in West Lothian which at that time provided the Duke with most of his expendable income. The dependence of the architectural activity on the profitable outcome of the industrial activity was made quite clear by the Duke in a letter to Adam of 6th January 1737:

> I am glad at last I hear better accts. Of my coal; perhaps it may turn out as you seem to flatter me it will; if so cubes, temples, obelisks, etc., etc. will go the better on.'

The second half of the exhibition dealt with Adam's achievements as a planner (a fascinating subject, dealt with in Ian Gow's paper) and garden designer, his important public works and his 'Last Years and Legacy'. In the first bay not only planning but also the decoration of rooms as well as the designing of gardens vied with each other for space. Almost inevitably, perhaps, the sheer quantity of material caused some confusion to creep into this section of the exhibition. Of necessity the views and plans of many of the houses were mixed together; a view of Haddo, for example, was juxtaposed with the interiors of Arniston and on all of my visits an unlabelled photograph of the dining room at Chatelherault was included among views of Torrance house.

Adam's work as 'Scotland's foremost designer of public buildings in the eary eight-eenth century'² was well represented in the exhibition with material relating to municipal buildings in Dundee, Haddington and Sanquhar, schools and hospitals in Edinburgh and the elegant library he designed for Glasgow University. His work for the Board of Ordnance was also dealt with, though one slightly puzzling item here was the inclusion of Inveraray Castle.

The final section on his late career and legacy was a delight, with an extremely interesting section on his protracted legal dispute with Lord Braco over Duff House and, what was for me the highlight of the exhibition, a superb model of the house as it would have been had it been completed to Adam's design. Another notable item here was the cast of the relief sculpture taken from the front of Adam's tomb. This is not normally visible through the gloom of the mausoleum and it was therefore a particularly welcome inclusion, especially since, in the background, there is a view of the building which provided the designers with the leitmotif of the exhibition lay-out, Chatelherault. What makes it particularly interesting is that it shows small but significant differences both from the engraving in Vitruvius Scoticus and from the building as it was completed a few years before Adam's death.

Overall, the exhibition was a great success in communicating both the diversity and quality of Adam's work. One of the major ways in which it achieved this was through the use of truly superb models of many of the key buildings, some of which have already been mentioned. The majority of these were by Simon Montgomery who deserves applause not only for the excellence of his models but also for the sheer perseverence and hard work that allowed him to produce so many in so short a time. They were particularly helpful in the case of buildings which have been demolished, like Gladney House, or, in reconstructing original intensions for buildings like Duff House, mentioned above. Similarly, the model of Mavisbank gave us some idea of what that sad ruin must have looked like when it was first built. Two other model makers also made a contribution. William Kay's House of Dun (which can now be seen in the house) was not originally made for this exhibition and was made at a far more leisurely pace than Simon Montgomery could afford. It is, in consequence, a very finely detailed work; its intricate mouldings even include the astragals on the windows and the roof is carefully sheathed with lead which I am reliably informed was obtained only after many bottles of wine had been drunk and the lead seals saved.

The model of Hamilton Parish Kirk was by David Adshead, who relied on his considerable skill as a painter to render the fine detail of the building. The steeple on this model is based on the engraving in *Vitruvius Scoticus* (Fig. 1) since the existing steeple is not by Adam and dates from the 1830s (it is, however, also derived from *Vitruvius Scoticus*). It is generally accepted, based on evidence in the Hamilton parish records that the present steeple replaced a timber one and that Adam's design was never executed. Recently, however, some new material has come to light which seems to contradict this and certainly shows that Adam produced an alternative design (Fig. 2) which is based on the steeple of Marylebone church in James Gibbs's *Book of Architecture* (Fig. 3). The drawing reproduced here is not in Adam's hand but is endorsed by his clerk of works at Hamilton, Robert Mein, and the Edinburgh wright, Archibald Chessels. The accompanying documents[3] show that in the spring of 1747 the steeple and some of the interior fittings 'have never as yet been begun to be built' and that the commissioners for the 6th Duke allowed £100 sterling for the completion of the work according to a plan 'refered to in the duke's obligation and drawn by Mr Adams and according to the estimate signed by Robert Mein, Mason. . .'. The following May, on the 13th, Mein and Chessels were sent back to report on the progress of the work and they 'reported their opinion that the steeple is sufficiently finished and execute according to the plan and that the sum of one hundred pounds sterling has been fully expended in executing the same.' They submitted detailed accounts which their endorsement makes quite clear refer to the drawing published here and through which we can identify at the very least the first two stages of this steeple, including the clock. The rest of the documents show that the heritors accepted that the kirk was 'completely finished conform to duke Hamilton's

1. The steeple of Hamilton Parish Kirk. From Vitruvius Scoticus, plate 13.

obligation and plan relative thereto.' The account for the work was finally settled in
September 1748.

So we end with something of a mystery. All of this seems to show quite clearly that,
despite widely accepted local wisdom, this steeple was built and, to retain a tenuous link
with my review of the exhibition, should have provided the basis of David Adshead's

2. (Robert Mein?) drawing after William Adam's design for Hamilton Parish Kirk steeple, c.1747/48.

3 The steeple of Marylebone Church. From James Gibbs, Book of Architecture (1728), plate 25.

model. However, the question remains; what happened to Adam's steeple and why was it necessary to replace it less than one hundred years after its construction?

John Lowrey, University of Edinburgh

ACKNOWLEDGEMENTS

I am grateful to the Duke of Hamilton for permission to publish the drawing of the steeple and to quote from the Hamilton Papers. Thanks are also due to Peter Vasey of the Scottish Record Office and to James Simpson.

NOTES

1. Hamilton Papers, Lennonxlove, Ex NRA(S)2177/872.
2. John Gifford. *William Adam, 1689–1748* (Mainstream 1989), p. 163.
3. The drawing and all the documents are in Hamilton Papers, Lennoxlove, Ex NRA(S)2177/F1/873.

John Douglas: William Adam's Rival?
Exhibition held at the National Monuments Record of Scotland, Edinburgh, 15 August–30 November 1989.

Until recently John Douglas was known only through his early drawings for the transformation of Blair Castle into a Gibbsian classical mansion. The recent discovery of a collection of his drawings, generously donated to the National Monuments Record of Scotland by the Edinburgh Company of Merchants, has allowed this important Scottish architect to emerge from obscurity and to act as a foil for William Adam's more spectacular career. The corpus can be confidently attributed to Douglas because of the stylistic resemblance to the Blair drawings and the inclusion of drawings for both Finlaystone and Archerfield, for which Douglas's contracts survive. The drawings, which reveal him as a competent, practical designer, are remarkable for their skilled penmanship and evocative use of washes. Engagingly, even rough sketches have been preserved, some of them drawn on old playing cards, apparently a ready source of scrap paper.

In his early years Douglas copied several plates from James Gibbs's *Book of Architecture*, including one copied by Gibbs from Palladio's treatise. Douglas perceptively recognised that Gibbs's happy combination of Palladian and Baroque elements offered a more robust classical model than the stricter Palladianism then in fashion in England. The NMR has been especially lucky to acquire Douglas's own copy of Gibbs's book, recently identified by Dr Terry Friedman. That Douglas was not a classical purist is shown by the beautiful drawing in the gothic style, perhaps connected with the Duke of Argyll's intention to rebuild Roseneath to match Roger Morris's neo-gothic proposals for Inveraray Castle. That he was also excited by geometry is clear from his octagonal design for Killin church, his ingenious use of central, toplit staircases and his curious elevation for an octapus-like villa with eight projecting square bays.

As Ian Gow's lively and erudite catalogue (free to visitors!) explains, Douglas, like Adam, was often employed to modernise existing structures, rather than to build new ones—Scottish eighteenth century landowners' architectural pretensions were rarely backed up by the wealth needed to start afresh. A number of his projects remained on the drawing board, as if in conformation of the patrons' economic constraints. It is ironic that the sober classicism of Douglas's modernised tower houses did not appeal to Victorian tastes or domestic needs, and several of his houses were re-gothicised (Dalhousie and Taymouth) or dwarfed by enormous extensions (Galloway House and Finlaystone). Sir Walter Scott was not impressed by Douglas's efforts at Dalhousie: 'the old castle was mangled by a fellow called, I believe, Douglas, who destroyed, as far as in him lay, its military and baronial character'.

Apart from the delight afforded by the drawings as works of art in their own right, the fascination of the collection lies in the way in which the architect's career can now be charted more confidently. Hitherto unattributed buildings such as Lochnell House in Argyll bear the distinctive trademarks of Douglas's work. It is particularly encouraging to see displayed his beautiful plan drawing for Archerfield House (Fig. 7 on p. 71), now threatened with complete remodelling for a hotel and leasure complex. This stately but sadly neglected house is commonly referred to as the work of Robert Adam, although nothing of Adam's work in the interior survives, simply because John Douglas is unknown and *everyone* has heard of Robert Adam.

Deborah Howard, University of Edinburgh